A WORLD WITHOUT WINDOWS

Living as a Christian
in a secular world

Derek Tidball

Scripture Union
130 City Road, London EC1V 2NJ

ISBN 0 86201 382 8

Phototypset by Input Typesetting Ltd, London.

Printed and bound in Great Britain by Cox & Wyman Ltd, Reading.

Contents

Page

Dedicated to
my friends at Northchurch Baptist Church,
Berkhamsted.

The reality of ordinary life is increasingly posited as the
only reality . . . The commonsense world becomes a world
without windows . . . Modernity produces an awful lot of
noise, which makes it difficult to listen to the gods.

Peter Berger
Against the World, For the World

Introduction

Secularization is a very difficult word! Everyone who uses it has his own idea as to what it means. Obviously it is important that we know what the user means when he uses it or we might misunderstand him. But attempts to come up with a generally agreed and precise definition seem to me quite pointless. Secularization is a varied and complex process that we meet in many different ways and places. So we shall happily use the word to describe a whole gamut of things. But what things?

One popular definition of secularization says that it is the process by which religious beliefs and practices lose their social significance. Religion, which was once at the heart of all life, loses control and even influence over many aspects of life. Some would say that the first secularization in England took place when the monasteries lost control of all that property under Henry VIII. Religion has been losing control and playing an increasingly marginalized part in social affairs, with periodic exceptions, ever since.

Some would want to argue that secularization is not a

bad thing. After all, relieving the monasteries of all that land released the monks to concentrate on the more religious aspects of their calling and saved them from a great deal of temptation from mammon. There is certainly an element of truth in such a view. The side-effects of secularization are sometimes helpful for the Christian. But on balance secularization is anything but helpful to Christian belief.

Examining it in greater depth we see that secularization is at work on the level of the individual, of society and its institutions, and at the higher level of culture. Individually, it means that fewer and fewer people go to church and that even the percentage of people who give positive religious answers in opinion poll surveys is decreasing. The practice and confession of religion is on the decline.

At the next level it means that society disengages itself from religion. So religion may still be wheeled out for state occasions but is actually a relic of the past. Religion is not really taught in schools any more and bishops, though they sit there, really have little influence in the House of Lords. Society, on the whole, operates on another basis. Religion, at best, lurks at its margins.

Culturally, we live in a world where it is harder and harder to believe in the supernatural dimension and where God never seriously crosses the mind of thinking or even unthinking adults. Our culture views the world as a closed system where resorting to God is never seriously considered.

Secularization means all these things and more. But it doesn't just take place 'out there', in the individual, in society or in the culture. It takes place in the church as well. The church all too easily conforms to the age in which it lives. So, put starkly, the real issues which concern it are material rather than eternal; the real way it operates is purely human rather than spiritual; and its reference points are horizontal rather than vertical. This is, of course, to oversimplify, for the true church must be concerned about God's created world in the here and now as much as God's plan of re-creation in the future. But the point is made; the balance has shifted.

Each of these aspects of secularization could be argued about at length. They are all debatable and need qualifying in a thousand ways. It is a pity that a whole mythology has been allowed to build up around the idea of secularization and that it is a widespread belief that religion is on its way out, soon to be heard of no more. For all its problems, however, Christians should not dismiss the idea of secularization too easily. The idea speaks of something which is real, if elusive, and gives us a number of signposts which help us to look further. In general terms we have to live out our Christian belief in a secular world – so we ought to know a little of what that means.

So much for secularization. What about secularism? Secularism is a much more pointed word. Secularization is a label for a complex social process, and those who use it do not necessarily think it a good thing. Secularism, on the other hand, is a philosophy which is committed to seeing the abolition of religion and the triumph of a godless, religionless world. Only a few are committed and informed secularists. But many of the ideas of secularism filter down and, at a more popular level, feed the progress of secularization. Our main concern in this book will be with secularization, although we cannot ignore secularism altogether.

I have written with a very specific objective in view. The aim is to reflect on our experience of secularization and see what the teaching of the Bible has to offer the Christian believer by way of help. In order to do that, in chapter one we begin to look at what our secular world is like. In chapter two we dig into the background of our world so that we can start to understand some of the ideas which have formed it. This chapter delves back into history, so some may wish to skip it. Personally, I think it provides us with an important perspective if we are to understand our present experience. Then, in chapter three, we accept that the idea is more complicated than any simple picture of secularization would admit and we begin to qualify the story.

In the next section, part two, we ask if the experience of people in the Bible bears any relation to our experience of secularization and find a number of points of identity both in the Old Testament (chapter four) and in the New (chapter five). With that as a background, in part three we look at the church today and examine the two-way relationship between the church and the world, and see the subtle inroads secularization has made (chapters six and seven).

Finally, in chapters eight and nine, which comprise part four of the book, we look at two passages of the Bible which have special relevance for the individual Christian believer living in an alien and unbelieving culture.

Some will be disappointed that we have not debated the validity of what sociologists say about secularization more than we have. It is a debatable concept. But the intention of this book has been different. For such people I would heartily recommend David Lyon's *The Steeple's Shadow* (SPCK, 1985). As a respected sociologist he engages more fully in the discussion about the concept of secularization. With a finely balanced hand he challenges some of the common assumptions, debunks some of the myths and, at the same time, challenges the church not to stick its head in the sand. It is a work of prime importance and readers who wish to take the matter further could not wish for a better starting-point than that.

Paul said that 'Everything that was written in the past was written to teach us, so that through endurance and the encouragement of the Scriptures we might have hope' (Rom 15:4). My prayer is that this book will prove the truth of his words for the believer struggling in a sea of secularism.

PART ONE

Looking at Ourselves

1
Living in a secular society

Take Robin...

On Sunday you will find Robin in church where he serves as an elder and sings in the choir. His hearty singing proclaims 'Jesus is Lord', and during worship he makes grand claims for God's justice, righteousness and power as creator and saviour. Likewise, he affirms that the Holy Spirit is God's active agent in the world today, enabling people to change and be born anew.

Monday to Friday, Robin is an accountant. When he goes into the office on Monday he basks in the warm glow of Sunday worship and feels sorry for those who could fill up their weekends only by watching Argyle or entertaining their mothers-in-law. But soon he's immersed in the hurly-burly of business life. Tough decisions have to be taken with clients about their investments. It seems that major profits are to be made by investing in manufacturing companies that exploit their workers and through property companies that will demolish whole communities to build more lucrative office blocks. Where, then, is the God who rescues 'the poor from those too strong for them, the poor and needy from those who rob them' (Ps 35:10)? The God of Amos is safely shut away in his Sunday closet. This is the real world.

On Tuesday it's prayer meeting night at the church and, as an elder, Robin must be seen there. The church is engaged in an evangelism programme at the moment and he prays about it. That's the most he can contribute to it because he's too busy to actually participate. He prays for the conversion of the people being visited. But he does not really pray with faith because, although he says he believes its power, he has had little experience of seeing the gospel at work in those near him. Come to think of it, he doesn't really believe the gospel has much power for those he works with because he doesn't really see it has too much relevance for them. They are nice, well-set-up folk who enjoy the security of living in their semis with their 2.4 children, 1.75 cars and index-linked pensions. For them, life seems quite self-contained. God, at best, is a God of the gaps who will squeeze into their lives only if something goes drastically wrong. But it probably won't – they are insured up to the hilt, have private medical policies and have purchased everything on the market to cushion them against the unexpected.

Back in the office on Wednesday, Robin has to deal with the Jasmine portfolio. It gives him a great deal of pleasure because he has cut a fair few corners for them and saved them an awful lot of taxes. In truth he has actually condoned quite a bit of tax evasion, but his conscience isn't permitted to remind him of that. After all, saving money is what he is paid for.

He also advises another company to turn a blind eye to the need to install expensive new machinery so that they no longer pollute the nearby river with their industrial effluent. It will be some time before the Health and Safety Executive catch up with them and, even though they know they are breaking the law and causing harm, he advises them to do nothing. 'Jesus is Lord, creation's voice proclaims it . . .' Well, so it might be – but not with Robin's help.

A third business deal is about to take place in the afternoon. He is about to sell a company on behalf of clients and he is not exactly honest in his discussion with the buyers. But he has to serve the interests of his clients and so a bit of lying here and there doesn't hurt. After all, it is common practice, everyone does it. It never crosses his mind that he is the disciple of a 'God who cannot lie'.

On Thursday it is the state of his own personal finances which occupies much of his thinking, and anxiously so. He's got to make a few preparations for the future to ensure that his family are secure. Money is juggled so that his boys can go to public school, his house can be extended and his pension keep pace with inflation. Finding security in the God who provided manna in the wilderness seems a little remote from the world in which Robin lives.

At the end of the week he has to suffer an elders' meeting. One of his fellow elders enthuses about a miraculous healing which has just taken place in someone he knows. Robin tries to share his enthusiasm but is a bit worried about the danger of fanaticism. Why couldn't the person just have gone to the hospital, had an operation and got healed in the normal way? That he would be able to cope with more easily.

When they get down to business they spend much of their time discussing the new building project and how to finance it. Some argue that faith is the key and they should call the church to prayer. Well, he can't argue against that. But what he really thinks, and what he says, is that they should make a widespread appeal to other churches, engage in a series of fund-raising activities and try to secure some cheap loans on the money market. Faith is all very well, but you have to be practical.

All week Robin has been living in two worlds and his thinking has been in separate compartments. His faith, so loudly proclaimed in the church, doesn't really affect his business life. But it could not be said that his business life doesn't affect his faith. God is great, if kept in a box.

It's not Robin's problem alone. He's just one person involved in a much more complex social process. What lies behind it? Let's broaden the picture.

From vertical to horizontal hold

The world in which we live has been described as a 'world without windows'. It is as if our world is a gigantic room surrounded by solid walls – a closed system which has no place for a supernatural dimension beyond the natural world.

Self-sufficiency
People don't see the need to look beyond the walls since everything they want is available within the room: they are self-sufficient. If something isn't on tap yet, the resources are present which will make it available one day.

If, as sometimes happens, someone wants to break out and look for realities or resources beyond the room, they are quickly brought back into line either by ridicule or the sheer weight of the social pressure which says there is nothing beyond. In such circumstances, even thinking about the possibility of knocking holes in the wall and looking outside the room to God is difficult.

The glimmerings of religion
For the vast majority of people today God is no longer a serious proposition and the supernatural is an irrelevance. But to say there are no windows is an exaggeration. At the big crisis points of life – birth, marriage and death – a flickering yearning for God and a nod in his direction might be acceptable.

There is also a sentimental attachment to religion in the minds of some since the church is good for children and old ladies. The church may even be quite useful in helping to produce a conformist society.

To some extent religion can be tolerated, but only because it is seen as a leisure activity chosen by the few, while others choose to play darts or support Everton or grow chrysanthemums. But once religion, the church, faith – call it what you will for the moment – impinges on the 'real' world it becomes immediately unacceptable. In practice, people chiefly live and think as if there is no God.

The Godward – manward shift of perspective

This world we inhabit, the one without windows, is not a sudden creation. It has developed over centuries. During that time the size of the windows has been gradually reduced until today they have almost, if not quite, disappeared.

There are indications of that reduction on every hand. Take art and music. Once most works of art or music were religious. Individual artists may not have been devout Christians, but their work was often under the patronage of the church and their themes consisted of religious scenes such as visions of heaven and hell.

Today a religious work of art is rare. Art is either devoted to cosy reproductions of this world or to reflecting the inner mind of the artist himself or, even worse, to reproducing the chaos and disease of the society around.

Music is the same. Once, virtually all music was church music. Now it is man-centred, so when 'Amazing Grace' or 'Kyrie eleison' get into the charts it is seen as odd and a matter for comment. The Christian musician who sings explicitly about his faith will be either on the receiving end of a good deal of unpleasantness or simply ignored.

Modern-day architecture reflects a similar shift in our culture. The skyline was once dominated by the towers and steeples of churches. Now these are dwarfed by the temples of commerce. London's NatWest Tower snootily looks down on the graceful dome of St Paul's Cathedral and stands as eloquent evidence that mammon seems more impressive than God.

Changes like these are not merely external. They have

deep implications for the way we think.

Centuries ago people deliberately built huge churches which stood above all else. That they pointed skywards was a conscious reminder of how God was over all and that men should look beyond themselves to him. They were elaborate and grand because God deserved the best.

If anyone today were so foolish as to suggest building churches on that scale they would be reminded that the world has millions of hungry mouths to feed and that poverty abounds everywhere. If there is any spare money it must go to charitable causes not to religious luxuries. Thus the vast Liverpool Cathedral, built this century, is considered an expensive white elephant in a city of poverty.

Even in the church, our thinking has become much more man-centred. Professor Charles Moule, a past professor of Divinity at Cambridge University, summed it up when he remarked, 'When I was an undergraduate the underlying message was "Come to Jesus", today it is "Give to Oxfam".'

Double-think

These changed thought-patterns often manifest themselves in double-think: what applies naturally in one sphere is alien to another. Christian businessmen often suffer from double-think. They apparently see no difficulty in opposing the spending of money on the church and its buildings while happily adding on storeys to their office blocks. Business demands it. Maybe, but the yardsticks they use to measure the morality of spending money in the business world and those they use for spending it in the church are very different. No one in the business world says the new building can't go ahead because the money must be given to the famine victims of Africa instead. It isn't just that commerce has grown and religion has shrunk: commercial and manward thinking is now central; religious and Godward thinking is peripheral.

Public and private worlds

Double-think is possible because people live in two worlds. First, there is the private world. Here all sorts of bizarre ideas may be entertained and practices indulged in. Then there is the public world where they may not. The public world defines what reality is. Ultimately it is this world which dominates our thinking. Religion has a place in the private world but it must not seriously affect the public world. If religion comes into play at all in the public world, it is expected to do no more than baptize it by agreeing with whatever the latest dictum is and by producing vague moral support for it. So a Remembrance Day ceremony is acceptable because it is a reminder that God was on our side. Similarly it is acceptable for a bishop to bless a nuclear submarine. But if an archbishop does not kowtow to current political opinion he is liable to receive a barracking and be told to keep his nose out of politics.

At one time the public world did recognize religion as a powerful force. Religious leaders had real influence in politics, and religious worship was a vital ingredient in education. Now the place of bishops in the House of Lords and the continued practice of school assemblies in British education are little more than cultural left-overs.

Today the real world is the world of political power, economic necessity and technological progress. Self-interest and the need to maintain power dictate choices in the real world, whatever the morality of a particular political action. So although the Bible says we should not put our trust in princes or in mortal men who are unable to save us (Ps 146:3), governments put their trust in the balance of conventional forces and in nuclear weapons like Cruise missiles. No moral argument which opposes them can have the slightest effect while the overriding concern is to ensure that the Eastern bloc does not get the edge in the arms race. Trust is no longer put in God, but in the theory of deterrence. There are times when morality does enter political judgments – relations with South Africa do not enjoy unrestricted freedom, because the policy of apartheid is abhorrent to many in the West – but where it does enter in it is often adulterated by self-interest and conveniently benefits one's own ends. Thus it is easy to be full of righteous indignation when one's own territory is invaded but to be silent when one's allies invade the territories of others. Righteousness is flexible.

In the real world, morality, whatever form it takes, tends to be tempered by economic reality. Hence, during the Falklands crisis all sorts of measures were adopted against Argentina, but economic links were sacrosanct. Even when the economic altar is removed and economic links are severed, plenty of ways are soon devised to enable men to go on worshipping at mammon's temple. Time and again morality gives way to economic expediency.

In the British Parliament, Christian MPs face difficult choices of conscience on issues relating to private and public morality. Whatever their private Christian views may be, they know they will not be heard if they stand in the House and quote scriptures. Only if good, sound economic or social reasons are advanced will their values be influential. This, and the issues mentioned above, illustrate how subtle shifts have entered the culture and made the atmosphere unconducive, if not hostile, to religion.

The forces that shape our world

What lies behind these 'subtle shifts' in our culture?

Technology
The biggest single factor is the mighty force of technology.

A couple of centuries ago it was essential that new inventions took place, simply to enable the rapidly expanding population to be fed and clothed properly. A romantic view of England prior to the industrial revolution is difficult to hold. There was much poverty and squalor, and an improvement in the quality of life was desperately needed for all but the rich. But new inventions brought with them their own price. They began to impose a new way of life and of thinking which was less favourable to faith. Technology introduced new imperatives, a new landscape and a new mind-set.

The implications of technology

By its nature, technology involves *a commitment to progress and growth*. It aims to improve the quality of life and it believes that there are no limits to the improvements which are possible. So by inventing apparatus which will help the sufferer, or drugs which will dull the pain, medical research can reduce the discomfort involved in certain illnesses. By its research it can successfully treat and control many diseases. The further development of preventative techniques can then eliminate them altogether. Life can be elongated and death projected further into the distance. Yesterday's killer diseases are unknown today and today's killer diseases will be unknown tomorrow. In the end, medical science will even be able to cure the common cold! Given sufficient time, research and resources, technology, it is believed, will be able to solve all the problems men face. There are no boundaries. Such unbounded confidence means, as Os Guinness has expressed it, that the universe is no longer a mystery to be penetrated but simply a Rubik's cube to be sorted out.

Every now and again the high priests of technology explicitly state that their confidence lies in man. On 21 September 1979, the *Daily Telegraph* carried a full page advertisement by BP. Most of the page was devoted to a picture of loaves and fish. The caption trumpeted, 'Feeding the five thousand . . . thousand . . . thousand.' Underneath, it read, 'The world grows at the rate of 175,000 extra mouths to feed, every day. To keep them fed can't depend on miracles, but on skill and technology.' Less than a month later another full page advertisement pictured a sandwich-board carrier announcing, 'The end is nigh' and 'Prepare to meet thy doom.' The end to which Taylor

Woodrow was alluding was not that of meeting God, but of running out of oil.

Technology is obviously a costly enterprise and consequently brings with it, at least in a capitalist society, *the need to minimize the costs involved*. This has implications for the methods which are acceptable. Whatever technology produces needs to be reproduced over and over again with a great deal of precision. There is little room, therefore, for craftsmanship, which is an expensive and individualized way of doing things. Rather, the process of production is reduced to a number of small, precise acts which can be exactly measured and repeated over and over. In this way people become specialists in their own particular operation, but at the same time highly dependent on everyone else.

Technology's methods of production involve *human costs* which are great but not always recognized:

• Man is reduced to something like a machine himself. Rather than being encouraged to reflect the image of God, who is a creator of infinite and colourful variety, the industrial worker is reduced to one operation on an assembly line with no opportunity for creating anything.

• His personal emotions are managed by the demands of the production process.

• He cannot take holidays when he wants to, still less when the calendar of the church demands it, but only when the machinery can be closed down.

• If the machinery demands it, he has to work in shifts, however disruptive that might be to family life.

• He is involved in anonymous social relationships. It does not really matter who he is as long as he serves the machine.

• Convenience dictates that he has to live in big urban areas rather than in scattered rural communities.

Modern man is locked into a system where interdependence is the key – people and operations are not autonomous, they depend on everyone and everything else – and where his survival can easily be threatened if things go wrong. A striking illustration of this point took place at 5.16 pm on

9th November 1965. At that moment two metal contacts touched at Niagara Falls and within twelve minutes the power cut had plunged the whole of the north-east of the United States into chaos. Thirty million people were affected. 800,000 people were trapped in subways; 250 flights had to be diverted from John F Kennedy airport; 150 hospitals were endangered, only half of which had emergency generators. This was all because a trip-switch designed to prevent the power supply system from being overloaded had been triggered. In fact it should have been upgraded years before and was set at too low a limit. What a frightening picture of man dependent on technology!

Information technology

With the coming of the current information technology revolution, these implications and costs have not changed; they have simply been confirmed.

Much of the drudgery of labour may disappear, but the confident belief in our ability to make progress, the devaluing of man and the problems of interdependence simply increase. Customers are no longer known by names but by numbers. And we all know of the horrifying stories of hugely inflated bills being received by frightened old ladies because of a blip on the computer. Such things would not happen in a more personalized world. Moreover, a problem with a central computer can wipe out valuable records, prevent you from getting money out of your account or even set the temperature of a department store's heating system at an uncomfortable level because it is being controlled hundreds of miles away. All of these render the person powerless.

Bureaucracy

Hand in hand with technology comes the need to organize, so bureaucracy has grown alongside technology. A massive labour force, mammoth production plants and research laboratories could not function but for that.

Bureaucracy exhibits the same confidence as technology

and, likewise, introduces a particular sort of mentality which is harmful to a spiritual interpretation of the world. Technology says that in the end any problem can be solved. Bureaucracy says that in the end any problem can be organized. But organization on this scale can only take place if certain principles are accepted.

The implications of bureaucracy
● We must believe that the world is orderly, routine and predictable. If it is not so already, we must make it so.
● We must accept that not everyone can take decisions. Those who do take them must be properly qualified to do so and certified as competent. So many plain, common-sense decisions which ordinary people used to make for themselves are now the domain of the official.
● There is a proper procedure to be followed which must not be ignored.
● People engaged in a bureaucratic process are supposed to be anonymous.

All these points can be illustrated if you think of a Social Security office. The belief is that poverty can be eliminated by use of the correct organization. But only those who have been properly trained and know the correct procedure can help to eliminate it. Furthermore, it has to be done in the correct way. The regulations have to be applied, the correct forms have to be completed and the office hours observed. Bad luck if you are poor outside the stated hours of business. What is more, it should not matter who the official is or who the person on the other side of the counter is. The same question should get the same answer no matter who is involved. So a person queuing up for his Social Security should get the same money whether the civil servant dealing with him is someone he has never met before or is his best friend. This anonymity is imperative if bureaucracy is to work.

The basic principle behind this stress on anonymity is a belief in justice and fairness. Men and women should be able to have their rights, as defined by Parliament, no matter who they are. If there is a hiccup in the system, and for some reason they are denied them, then there must be a tribunal or court to which they can appeal for redress.

It is generally accepted that people have rights and that they should be encouraged to pursue them. Of course, people do not realize that a world of justice and fairness like that, ruled over by human beings, is very tyrannical. It's tyrannical, not least because it depends on who makes up the rules as to what is just and fair.

Commitment to the principles of justice and fairness also cuts at the root of a spiritual interpretation of the world. Job spent the time of his illness pleading for justice, only to discover, in the end, that it would not help him. What he needed was grace. Many came to Jesus asking for mercy, because justice would have left them to stew in their misery. The Christian view is that the world is governed by a personal God who abounds in love. But that does not fit comfortably with a bureaucratic view of the world. Bureaucracy finds grace untidy.

Pluralism

At a practical level we live in a plurality of worlds and we are also confronted by a plurality of different world-views.

People used to live in a single world. They lived over the shop or, at least, in the community where they worked. They were, and were seen to be, integrated people. Family, commercial, political and religious behaviour and attitudes were evident for all to see. And they reinforced each other.

But this is no longer so. We now live in several worlds which may not relate to each other at all. And we touch on several other worlds, all of which operate according to a different world-view, that is, according to a different set of values, expectations, understandings and interpretations of life. All this militates against a unified world-view.

At the simplest level, most of us live in two worlds: the world of work and the world of leisure. Urbanization has forced us to do so. And the two often do not relate at all.

A dramatic illustration of this division can be seen in a

man like Dennis Nilsen. In his nine-to-five world he seemed a perfectly ordinary civil servant, doing his duty in a quite unremarkable way; but outside of office hours he was committing numerous sexual offences and murders. A Jekyll and Hyde existence is all too possible.

Usually of course, the dichotomy between the public and the private does not have such dramatic consequences. But it has enabled us to take the teaching of religion less seriously by ensuring that it is seen merely as a private matter.

Pluralism is, however, a good deal more complicated than that. It is enshrined in our way of life as a good thing.

Education

From early days, the school child will have his views challenged and questioned. His parents may have taught him certain values or a particular faith, but he will be encouraged by his education to doubt it and constantly revise it. Looking at other people's viewpoints, seeing something from another's standpoint and understanding the experience of someone very different are all valued highly.

The worst crime that can be committed in a school essay is to be dogmatic and sweeping in your statements. Things need to be qualified and bets need to be hedged.

To be sheltered and innocent, not to have been exposed to a wide range of experiences in life, is frowned upon as a weakness. Indeed, it has been known in extreme cases for the social services to take children into care if the upbringing provided by the parents has been considered by the courts to be too restrictive.

The media

The media aids the pluralism process enormously. All day long the public are bombarded with a multiplicity of information, much of which is contradictory. The choice of channels through which the information comes is legion. And although certain channels may broadly espouse a certain viewpoint, the media as a whole is devoted to letting different interpretations have their full share of the limelight.

If there is an IRA bombing in Northern Ireland, the media will not only interview the police and armed forces but will give time to the view of the IRA, seeking, if possible, to broadcast an interview with one of their spokesmen.

The open-ended chat show, where no verdicts are reached and no one wins the debate, is the arch symbol of a media committed to openness. Only intolerance cannot be tolerated.

Programme planners ensure that time is given to a host of minority viewpoints with the result that the media is in danger of presenting an unbalanced picture of national life. Good news is not considered to be newsworthy and stable marriages don't make for good drama. So it is the bad and the ugly that dominates the screen. Experts are called in to discuss issues – and they are given all of three minutes to settle profound issues and, *en route*, to fully expose the disagreements they have with each other.

Increasing openness

Following the Second World War, life became more and more open. Gone were the days when sons followed in their fathers' footsteps as far as work was concerned. New opportunities, which previous generations had never dreamt of, opened before the post-war generation. Career prospects were simply not as fixed.

The expansion of higher education gave many who previously would not have stood a chance the possibility of post-school learning, and with the expansion of places at university came the expansion of horizons.

The improvement in travel further facilitated this expansion. Seeing the world and visiting other cultures was no longer the privilege of the rich. Travel, of course, was a two-way street, for not only could we visit other places, others could visit us and even settle among us. The increased number of immigrants, from places which were not just a replica of Britain, brought other faiths and cultures to our doorstep.

The implications of pluralism
This openness is both exciting and frightening. For many it can lead to maturity. But its effect can equally be to make modern man's mind homeless, and that can be a terrifying condition to be in. It has been described as giving man a permanent identity crisis. We cannot settle on firm convictions or believe confidently in dogmas any more. No sooner have we sorted out what we think we believe than someone else comes along and causes us to revise our position. So just when we think we know what we think about apartheid in South Africa, we listen to another documentary, giving an alternative viewpoint, and our view is blown wide open again.

Pluralism encourages people to switch allegiance. Many people are into God in their teens, into politics in their twenties, into families in their thirties and never carry over anything from one decade to the next. Membership of groups and societies is fleeting and fickle. And commitment to beliefs is even more so. Truth cannot be firmly held. All we can do is hold opinions provisionally. It is immediately apparent how opposed this is to a Christian faith that is based upon a God who reveals himself as truth.

Summary

In our secular society the focus of man's attention has shifted from heaven to earth, from God to man. In doing so man has created a world where God has been squeezed out and where it is not only increasingly difficult to believe in God but also increasingly unnecessary to do so. We feel that the real world is the world of the everyday life that we see about us. Technology and bureaucracy have made God implausible, which is bad enough. But they exist in the context of pluralism, and that is worse, for it shakes modern man's confidence in his ability to believe in anything for sure.

2
How did we get here?

Robin, our 'two-worlds' Christian accountant and church elder, lives in a world where science and technology reign, where individualism is prized above all else in spite of pressure to conform to general secularist attitudes, and where religion is no longer a vital part of the community but a private hobby. How did this world come about?

If you are looking for a scapegoat there is an obvious one to hand. In 1866 Charles Bradlaugh founded the National Secular Society which was committed to doing away with religion. Following Bradlaugh's example a number of societies were formed which had secular or humanist aims. But they never attracted huge memberships. Even today, a group like the British Humanist Association, formed in the 1960s by amalgamating a number of older societies, has only a few thousand members. But as with many scapegoats, if you were to attack Bradlaugh, the real culprits would escape.

Only a few might be committed to the philosophy of secularism but many will be caught up in the process of secularization. The two phenomena are obviously closely related, but not in any simple way. It is too easy to say that the former caused the latter. It works both ways round. That is why attacking Bradlaugh as a scapegoat might be to attack the wrong target. Secularism contributes to secularization and secularization contributes to secularism. Our eyes need to be open to both.

So how did our secularized society with its belief in secularism really come about? Normally it is explained by looking at the intellectual ideas which gave rise to secularist thinking. These *are* important and this approach is the best way to start our investigation. But it is not the only factor, as we shall see.

Intellectual factors: the rise of secular ideas

In the seventeenth century people accepted two sources of authority, the Bible and the classics, and these dominated their cultural horizons. But during the eighteenth-century Enlightenment they were increasingly questioned and people lost confidence in them. A number of trends combined to make this so.

The rise of experimental science

Francis Bacon (1561 – 1626) introduced the method of experiment to science. This technique seemed capable of distinguishing truth from error. Its use meant that things no longer had to be accepted simply on the basis of tradition. Isaac Newton (1642 – 1727) established Bacon's approach by proving its value. Consequently it became the foundation of the modern scientific approach. This new way of looking at things implied that human reason was capable, through careful observation, of revealing the mechanisms of natural law. The poet Alexander Pope neatly summed it up in an *Epitaph* for Sir Isaac,

Nature and Nature's law lay hid in night:
God said, 'Let Newton be!' and all was light.

The implications of the scientific method

The early scientists were devout Christians who began experimenting precisely because they believed God had created an ordered creation. But they led the world into thinking that God was a sort of grand mathematician whose results were accessible to man, rather than a mystery who could not be probed.

Inevitably, too, the stress on there being a regular order which could be observed, led to more and more emphasis being put on the providence and goodness of God and less and less on the fall of man and evil in the world. Obviously, such a re-emphasis changed the traditional view of the relationship between God and man, tending to make man less dependent on God.

The scientists also championed the right of free enquiry and did so in the face of religious authority. Eventually this meant that Newton's scientific approach could be adopted while his Christian framework could be discarded.

The theory of evolution

By the mid-eighteenth century the extraordinary rise of science was on its course. But in the mid-nineteenth century it was to reach a new level of conflict with religion over the theory of evolution. Charles Darwin (1809 – 1882) with his famous *On the Origin of Species* (1859) is the symbol or occasion of the conflict rather than its cause, despite what Christians so often seem to think. Evolutionary thinking was already established as a general philosophy. Sociologists, for example, had long taught that the world was progressing all the time to higher levels of existence. What Darwin did was to provide that general philosophy with an apparent scientific basis and therefore a firmer authority. In the popular mind Darwin had proved that science was in conflict with Christianity. In fact, of course, it was not so. Men like T H Huxley (1825 – 1895) popularized Darwin's views because they could be used against religion. People latched on to them as ready allies in their general disillusionment with religion, not because they were really interested in science. There is little evidence that genuine scientists were led into doubt because of Darwin. Michael Faraday, Lord Kelvin and Joseph Lister are just a few of the eminent scientists who continued firm in their faith. No matter, in the popular mind – which was already unsettled about faith – science had disproved the truth of religion, therefore religion could safely be left behind.

The idea of progress
Closely related to the theory of evolution was the idea of progress. Men felt that religion had imprisoned them in the status quo. If the chains of religion could be removed, man would become free to rebel against his lot in life and change and improve it, rather than just accept it. So people became much more man-centred in their thinking. Again, Alexander Pope expresses the spirit of his age so well. In his *Essay on Man* written in 1733 he says:

> Say first, of God above, or Man below,
> What can we reason, but from what we know?
> Of man, what see we but his station here,
> From which to reason, or to which refer?

> Know then thyself, presume not God to scan,
> The proper study of mankind is Man.

It was confidently believed that this concentration on man himself would lead to an improvement in life because man was basically good. The 'fall' was dismissed as a fanciful story which took place before recorded history and had no real significance.

Man was a capable being who now took the centre of the stage and pushed God into the wings. Progress would occur simply because man loved himself. And it would not go astray because he was a rational and sensible being who would save himself from falling into too many holes or going down too many blind alleys. Pope again captures it well,

> Two principles in human nature reign,
> Self-love to urge and Reason to restrain.

The direction of man's thinking had changed. Previously he had looked to the past, – to tradition, age, experience; to the classics for wisdom, and to scripture for his authority. Now he looked to the future. He believed he had within his own hands the power to shape his tomorrows. That was where he was going to invest his efforts and resources.

It was not only the natural sciences which were to do this but the social sciences as well. Sociology grew out of the breakdown of society which took place during the French Revolution. It was a response to the urgent need to rebuild society. And men confidently believed that they could do so. In all their early writings sociologists demonstrated this belief in their ability to determine what the social future was going to be. The backward look had given way to the forward look.

The understanding of history
During the nineteenth century, history became organized as a proper academic discipline and overcame some of the naive thinking from which it had suffered. Not until 1866, for example, when William Stubbs was appointed Regius Professor of history at Oxford University, did it become a serious subject there. Even later Charles Kingsley, the Regius Professor at Cambridge, still adopted the old approach and thought that history was there to provide moral instruction, to illustrate the conflict between God and evil and to ensure that people realized that wickedness got its just deserts.

The modern approach was much more detached. The modern historian learnt to investigate what happened without preconceived ideas and without trying to prove a certain moral point. This demanded that he look at the evidence in a new way. He would not take it at face value but would investigate its trustworthiness and assess its relative significance. He would then seek to write his conclusions from an objective standpoint.

The significance of this for Christianity lay in the fact that Christianity claimed to be based on the historical life of Jesus. The nineteenth century saw a new debate open up about how reliable the picture of Jesus was. People like D F Strauss (1835) and E Renan (1863) began to call into question the trustworthiness of the Gospels as historical documents.

The Gospels did, after all, include a fair number of miraculous elements which did not easily relate to the world of the nineteenth century where miracles, to say the least, were not common. Perhaps they were mythical elements used by the early Gospel writers to express profound ideas, but not accurate records of actual events. Once this process had begun, a whole barrage of objections was raised against the reliability of the Bible. Confidence in the foundation of Christianity began to crumble and many were led into a position of scepticism.

New views of knowledge

The scientific, social and historical developments went hand in hand with developments in thinking about knowledge.

During the period which found its climax in the writings of the philosopher Immanuel Kant (1724 – 1804), man's reason was seen as more and more important. Knowledge was no longer considered to derive from some outside source but to be the result of man's own mind exercising itself on the world around it. Anything that could not be known like this was to be doubted. Man's reason therefore became the ultimate umpire as to what man should believe or reject.

From the time when John Locke wrote his book *The Reasonableness of Christianity* (1695) through to the nineteenth century, many theologians devoted themselves to trying to prove that Christianity was a reasonable faith. Philosophical arguments and natural revelation became the grounds on which they now attempted to build Christianity. But such grounds were shaky. Not only could others produce counter-arguments but their arguments for God always seemed to stop short of the God of the Bible. Religion within the limits of reason alone seemed ill-equipped to deal with the dimension of the supernatural or even with a God of grace, for grace by definition means unreasonable love.

Although the more recent philosophy of existentialism has reacted against cold reason and insists that what an individual subjectively feels is more important, the reign of reason still continues largely unopposed. People no longer believe because external authority tells them they must. They believe only what can be proved by experiment, observed by the eye or argued by the mind. They have set up their own minds as the final judge of what is true.

Religious factors: religion digs its own grave

The windows of our world were not reduced in size only by intellectual advances. Ironically religion itself may have contributed to a secular view. Again it is a complex picture, but four historical episodes will illustrate the point.

The Old Testament

The Jewish religion was different from many ancient faiths in that it distinguished between the sacred and the secular. Virtually the whole book of Leviticus is concerned with the issue, and numerous illustrations can be found there. Certain things and actions were considered clean and holy while certain others were considered unclean and profane.

By doing this the Jews created a framework where it was possible for people to begin to think and behave in a secular fashion. Such a possibility does not exist, say, in Hinduism. There the absence of any distinction between the religious and the secular means that economics, politics, science and so on are all inevitably seen in a religious and not an independent perspective.

But it was more than this. The Jews also believed in just one God. The world was not populated on every street corner by a different god, nor was every stream, tree or strange place inhabited by a petty and unpredictable deity. There was one God over all, who was distanced from his world and yet involved with it. His involvement was usually regular and orderly. Day and night, light and darkness, seed-time and harvest could be relied upon to follow one after the other. Of course, God could and did occasionally interrupt the orderliness of the world with some form of supernatural intervention but this was not an everyday occurrence.

This predictability of the world reduced the element of mystery which other religions encouraged. Many religions presented the world as if it were an enchanted garden in which people were akin to little children who were wondrously overawed by what they had seen. Not so the Jewish people. Their world was much more disenchanted than that. But that opened up the possibility that man would assume his own independence.

The crisis of the Reformation

Christianity owes much to the Old Testament and has inherited the legacy of disenchantment from it. It was because of this that Christians were the original and best scientists. But their own history has also served to encourage secularism.

Before the Reformation there was in the West essentially one interpretation of reality which, although individuals may not have fully believed in it, was widely accepted. The Reformation was a crisis of authority; it separated religion from culture, made religion a more individual matter and introduced people to the possibility of choice. Before the rupture that took place through the challenge of Martin Luther, people had no choice. From then on they had the possibility of choosing between, at least, Protestant and Catholic. With the introduction of that choice there came the possibility too that people would choose to remain on the sidelines and not be involved at all. Once that happened, agnosticism and atheism became real options. The seeds of pluralism were replanted by the Reformation.

The Puritan ethos

Another feature of the Reformation, which was heightened even more by the Puritans, was that Christianity was made a religion of the book. The place given to the Bible gave Protestantism the character of being learned, and a great stress was placed on the mind. Doctrine rather than experience became the real test of religious faith.

Among the doctrines emphasized by the Puritans was that of election. God had chosen some to salvation and their election depended totally on grace. There was nothing a man could do to earn it, and equally there was nothing he could do to prove that he was elect. That, as the German sociologist Max Weber was the first to point out, had an interesting effect on his personality.

Since a person could never be sure of his election, the only thing he could do was to live as if he was among the elect and show in his behaviour the fruits you would expect of the elect.

Given their powerful view of God, as one who was holy, transcendent, all-demanding and orderly in his creation, they lived lives which matched. They saw *all* people as called to please God, not just those who entered a religious profession. So all life had to be lived for the glory of God. Sins of the flesh had to be avoided, resources had to be cared for and accounted for carefully, orderliness was prized and superstition banished.

They were stewards of God's world and therefore had to master and subdue it. All this demystified the world even more. But it also had other effects. It produced just the type of personality which was suitable to establish modern rational capitalism. The Puritan businessman would not shut up shop when he felt like it or spend all the profits getting drunk. In fact, because the flesh was not to be indulged, he would have little to do with his money except reinvest it, or give it away – but there might be other objections to that.

Whether the Puritans were responsible for founding modern capitalism is much disputed. But certainly other effects of their faith can be observed.

Curiously, being one of God's chosen ones, even though you could not be sure about it, led to a tremendous self-confidence. If you were God's man you could withstand the world – and some of them did. In England, for example, the Puritans were the ones who opposed the divine right of kings and challenged their authority, even to the extent of executing their monarch. No one else would have dared. But their beliefs enabled them to be significant catalysts in bringing about a more modern world in politics, science and economics.

The dissenting churches and the fight for liberty

Another period of Christian history has also contributed to making our world more secular. Following the Methodist revival of the eighteenth century, the dissenting churches also experienced a considerable rejuvenation. The government tried to suppress them through restrictive laws and this provoked them into becoming the champions of liberty.

An early victory came in 1812 when they were permitted to have freedom of worship, providing their places of worship and ministers were registered. But throughout the main part of the century the dissenters were fighting to overcome their disabilities in everything from education to burial rights.

Again, however, their fight for freedom could not be restricted to fighting for their own interests. Their freedom meant that others should have freedom too. So their action set off a trend which in the longer run was harmful to the very thing for which they stood. The liberalism with which they were so much associated politically was a liberalism which would eventually extend to the existence of religion itself and mean that the rights of those who were opposed to religion had to be respected as much as those who wanted to advocate it.

In all these ways, therefore, religion has become its own grave-digger. It did not set out to create a more secular world. It set out to create a world more favourable to its own religious position. And we rejoice in the freedom it brought about. But the unfortunate side-effect has often been anything but what was envisaged.

Social trends

To these intellectual and religious factors we must add a whole range of other factors, social, political and economic, which not only have an enormous effect in shaping our world but also exert an enormous influence on how we think about our world.

Pre-industrial society

Before industrialization most people lived in small communities and their thinking was dominated by the locality in which they lived. It was a highly structured community in which everyone knew his place, for the rungs on the social ladder were clearly marked.

At the top would have been the squire and, close to him, the parson. The civil establishment and the ecclesiastical institution went hand in hand. The church was essentially a social institution which, while it may not have provided spiritual satisfaction, acted as a reasonably efficient administrative arm and welfare agency of the state.

The tight control exercised by the church can be seen in a thousand little ways such as the fact that in the early nineteenth century a quarter of all Justices of the Peace were clergymen. It was no wonder that there was a good deal of anti-clericalism around. Even so, those lower down were highly dependent on those above and needed to keep in their good books. It was important for them that they should conform both in their civil lives and in their religion.

Population growth

The growth of population was to change all that. In nineteenth-century England and Wales the population quadrupled and new patterns of living just had to develop. The changes took place from about 1760 onwards and meant that people moved from villages to towns and from the south and east to the north and west. The old parish structure simply couldn't cope with the change. Parish boundaries were inappropriate to the new towns which found that they did not have churches in the right places. This had implications even for national government since it could no longer rely on the parish structure as a ready-made administrative system.

Class structures

From this period on, the church in Britain never had the support of the working classes. Church was something which was alien to the worker's way of life. It lay outside his experience. It belonged to the middle and upper classes. The wealthy went to the Anglican churches and the modestly prosperous went to the Free churches but the working man largely went nowhere.

A survey in the *Daily News* in 1903 established the close link between social class and church attendance. In the poorest areas only 11.7% of the population attended church; in the mid-middle class areas it was 22.7% while in the wealthy suburban areas it was as high as 33.8%.

The working classes had a warm culture of their own which, although it took their own brand of morality seriously, did not take religion seriously. Generosity came before honesty; sympathy before truth and love before chastity. It was respectable people who went to church, and any member of the working class who went probably had aspirations above his status. To go to church meant you had to dress up, and most people didn't have the right clothes to wear. If you did go, you made yourself an obvious social nonconformist. City missionaries found the vast majority of the working classes indifferent to their spiritual state. They were not so much secularist as just blasphemous and irreligious. Working-class communities were bounded by a high wall and the church was on the other side of it.

Political developments

With the growth of this new class system came the growth of new political parties. Voting rights were extended in 1832 and again in 1867, giving the middle classes more political power. With that came the growth of Liberalism which held special significance in the nineteenth century and almost became a byword for the time.

The nineteenth century was pro-liberty. In 1859 John Stuart Mill (1806 – 1873) wrote a book, *On Liberty*, which was the theme of the age. The quest for liberty was greatly enhanced by the development of the printing press and the growth of journalism. Through them liberal opinions could be distributed to the farthest village in the land and their popularity could be greatly increased. And they were.

Liberalism owed much, as we have seen, to nonconformity, and much of it had a religious philosophy at base. But, as we have also seen, in the end it proved a powerful secularizing force. It was not anti-religious as such, it was just pro-liberty. But two things made it anti-religious in the end.

Firstly, when liberty is the goal it is difficult to know where to draw the line. Liberty for the religious is fine, but what about liberty for those of a different religion or of no religion? Secondly, the quest for liberty was a suitable bandwagon for others to join who were not motivated by the greater glory of God but by their own secular ends. Political forces which were ultimately to lead to secularization had therefore been unleashed.

Economic trends

Community changes

Economic changes also had their effect. As industry developed in the late nineteenth and early twentieth centuries, there was the need for more capital and consequently for new commercial procedures. The focus of industry therefore had to shift from being personal and local to being national and governmental. This had wholesale implications for the community life of the towns. Until these changes took place, many of the important businessmen lived locally and were key figures in supporting a whole range of voluntary and religious activities. But the dictates of capitalism moved them out of those localities, and their financial and personal support for local groups began to diminish.

The impact on leisure

It was not just that management was now undertaken by bureaucrats and professionals, and that the labour forces became more self-conscious and unionized. It was that the vice-president of the football club or of the Band of Hope was no longer as available as once he was. So survival for these and a host of other voluntary groups and societies depended on their becoming more organized. Rather than just blending in as part of the social scenery they now had to have membership lists so that they could count on the loyalty and support of some and exclude others from benefiting on the cheap. With membership came the need for rules and the need to satisfy the membership, so a much more professional attitude and the need to present an attractive programme grew.

You can see all this clearly in the history of a number of football teams. While they may once have been content to play in any old strip on a piece of ground which was open to all, gradually they start to build fences, charge gate money, have a posh team identity, aim to own full-time players, transfer them in from elsewhere and so on. The natural community base of this leisure activity was eroded and football became a specialized activity which one had consciously to opt into.

The same forces had their effect on religion. Rather than being a natural part of the fabric of the community it became a more professional activity which some opted into while the majority no longer bothered, or perhaps could no longer afford to bother. In fact, in comparison with other leisure activities, religion fared reasonably well. But it was to be affected in the longer term.

Religion was now a leisure activity chosen by a few while others chose any number of other leisure activities. The range of leisure activities was of course greatly increased. It has often been said that the development of the railways might be more responsible for the emptying of the churches than almost anything else. The railway brought the seaside or the country park within the reach of many people, and the idea of 'the weekend' began to grow.

In the twentieth century, with the development of the consumer society, leisure has become less social and more privatized. Why go to a football match when you can get a much better view of the game on the TV at home? The hi-fi, telephone, TV, video and press, together with DIY, and so on, make entertainment increasingly home-centred. Such trends, which had their roots in economic necessity, are all unhelpful to religion and a religious world-view.

The idea of improvement

Another aspect of these economic trends is the commitment to improvement. Capitalism is based on making a profit, some of which can then be reinvested to make an even greater profit. It believes that we should be engaged in a never-ending endeavour to make more and make better.

That economic philosophy spills over into all life. On a personal level, we believe that our standard of living should be greater this year than last. On a social level, we believe that it is the duty of government to improve the quality of our lives to an ever-increasing degree.

Historically the major outworking of this attitude is to be found in the welfare state. It is committed to making life more comfortable through education, health and social services. In many ways it reduces the insecurities of life.

Most obviously it reduces the insecurities involved in homelessness or unemployment by providing ways, albeit inadequate, in which the threat of those desperate conditions are cushioned. Less obviously it distances the biggest threat which all of us face, that of death. It does this by increasing longevity through medical research. In 1680 the average person could expect to live just twenty-nine and a half years. By 1975 the average man could expect to live until he was sixty-nine and the average woman until she was seventy-five.

No one in their right mind would decry these great humanitarian improvements. But again, it must be said that they have a spiritual cost. They not only produce a better world in which to live but change our way of thinking about the world. They encourage 'hubris', that insolent pride in life which puts man at the centre of his thinking and which makes him attribute all his achievements to himself. Hubris is a temptation as old as Moses. He warned the children of Israel of it as they approached Canaan: 'You may say to yourself, "My power and the strength of my hands have produced this wealth for me." But remember the Lord your God, for it is he who gives you the ability to produce wealth . . .' (Deut 8: 17,18).

Summary

In this chapter we have done more than simply trace the intellectual, religious, political, economic and social forces which shape our modern secular world. We have also implicitly mentioned the ambiguity of secularization. On the one hand the gap left for God to fill has been diminishing and the windows which enable us to look out to him have been growing smaller. On the other hand many of the things which are now detrimental to faith had their origin in religion and many aspects of progress and modernity are the outworking, several generations later, of religious faith.

We should not be negative and obscurantist. We should thank God for the technological progress and the improvement in health and social conditions from which we all benefit. Yet, at the same time we must be aware of the spiritual costs which seem inherent in the forces which have moulded our modern world.

3
Is it so simple?

The picture we have painted so far is one in which the fortunes of religion are declining and a religious interpretation of the world is increasingly unusual. Although we have admitted that this tendency has always been evident, we have argued that it was greatly accelerated from the eighteenth century onwards. But this is very much a rough-and-ready picture – a crude portrait by any standards. Is it so crude as to be untrue? To this one-dimensional and colourless depiction we now want to add some colour and some depth and see if they substantially alter the picture.

Looking back to history

Those who argue that the world is less religious now than it was can only do so if they have some baseline in mind. If it is less religious now than it was, when do they consider it to have been more religious? That is an embarrassing question for many of the advocates of the secularization thesis.

Suggested religious high-water marks

The Victorian era
Some of them point to Victorian Britain as the summit from which we have declined. But while it may be true that we are not a church-going people to the extent we were in Victorian Britain, that is a very short time span in which to argue that secularization has taken place. And there are other problems with taking Victorian Britain as the benchmark by which we measure what is happening today.

Firstly, the same people who argue that Britain has been secularized during that time, as indicated by declining church attendance, face problems when they look across the Atlantic to the USA. Church-going there is extraordinarily high, possibly even higher than it ever was at the peak of Victorian Britain. So to talk of secularization there must mean something a bit different.

Secondly, why should you adopt the Victorian era as your bench-mark? If you adopted a slightly earlier time – say before the Wesleyan Revival – you might find that religion has increased rather than decreased.

Thirdly, is church attendance the real measure of what was taking place in Victorian Britain, or for that matter at any other time? True, church attendance was relatively high, but so was immorality, even if it was less obvious. The real situation was not nearly so straight forward. The *Royal George* turned turtle in a squall at Spithead (admittedly at the earlier date of 1782), and fourteen hundred lives were lost. What is interesting is that among the losses were not only 400 Bibles, taken on board for the crew's spiritual welfare, but also 400 prostitutes, taken on board for their physical comfort! The real situation is ambiguous and difficult to measure with any confidence.

The Constantinian era
To overcome these problems, others measure secularization by using earlier bench-marks. Some measure it from the time when the emperor Constantine adopted Christianity

as the official religion of the Roman Empire some time after AD 312. Yet masses of the population then either never adopted Christianity, and continued to believe in the old pagan gods, or adopted it as a matter of social convenience rather than for genuine motives. It is difficult to measure how genuinely Christian the world is at any one time, but it is unlikely to have been a good deal more genuinely Christian then than now.

The Middle Ages

A similar problem arises if the Middle Ages are chosen as the reference point.

That time may have publicly adopted Christianity and roughly founded its way of life on the Roman Catholic Church, but what real effect that had on the average person's belief is difficult to determine. We do know that superstition was widespread and pre-Christian myths circulated. They probably reflected the real beliefs of people more accurately than did official Christianity. That, it must be agreed, makes the West a more religious world then than now, but it proves very little of significance to the Christian.

Discounting a mythical high-water mark

The truth is that there have always been two tendencies running through man's experience – one to the secular and one to the sacred. There have always been comings and goings; times when more and times when fewer people went to church; times when the world was seen through more sacred eyes and times when it was seen through more secular eyes. It all depends when you start measuring as to what conclusion you come to, and it is too easy to fix the questions so that you get the results you want. Reality is a good deal more complex than is admitted by the theory that the world is becoming increasingly secular.

If today we seem to be living in a more secular period than some earlier periods, it is important that Christians admit and face it. But even so, that fact would not prove that Christianity is on the way out. To conclude that, you would have to believe that the future holds no surprises. But that would not be true to experience. Historians, with hindsight, may have read the signs which could have predicted the founding of Christianity, the coming of the Reformation or the onslaught of the Wesleyan Revival, but people living at the time did not. This view of secularization being on the increase assumes that Christianity is going to the dogs. But, as has been well said, it has apparently gone to the dogs many times before – and it has always been the dog which died!

The idea that the world was once much more sacred than it is now gives a rosy-coloured view of the past. It builds on the idea of a mythical golden age which probably never really existed. A more detailed probing of the past would lead to a much more mixed view of how people saw the world. And so would a more detailed view of the present.

Looking around today

While no one today would say the church still has the influence it once enjoyed in society, it is equally true to say that it still does have influence. The statements of bishops and archbishops are capable of making front-page news and of causing concern to the Government. Of course, the statements made or positions adopted by them may not please you and me but that does not detract from the fact that they have influence. Similarly, on the local level, the church or the minister can and often does exercise a fair degree of influence on certain policies. But judged by this alone, we would still need to say that our world is largely a secular world since their influence, though real, is very limited. But there is a whole range of religious expression and interest outside the walls of the official church which must also be taken into account.

Folk religion

Many people who never regularly go anywhere near a church exhibit some form of religious belief. It may be a 'folk religion' and it may be considered by those on the inside to be very impure and even idolatrous. But it is quite common and it must erect a big question mark over any argument which says that the world today is secular. What is this 'common religion' like?

It certainly does not subscribe to a coherent set of doctrines or beliefs. Far from it. It is a jumble of ideas which often contradict each other. But it is only the committed Christian who feels that they need sorting out. These ideas involve the feeling that you need to say you belong to a church, even though you never go. 'I'm a Methodist, but I don't go', or even more, 'I belong to the Church of England, but I never go', is a frequent response met by any door-to-door evangelist. People feel the need of a religious identity. What they mean is that was the church where they went to Sunday school, or where they got married, or where they feel they belong even though nobody in the church might recognize them. As John Betjeman puts it,

> . . . and though for the church we may not seem to care,
> It's deeply part of us, thank God, it's there.

For the practitioners of common religion, belief has little to do with church attendance. 'You can be a Christian without going to church' is a constant cry. What it does have to do with is ethics. Religion is about the golden rule, about doing as you would be done by. That's why Sunday school is good for the kids. It socializes them into society, but once the monster element in them has been tamed it has little more to offer.

While the institutional church may not score very highly in the minds of these people, personal prayer does. In our society an extraordinary number of people pray, even quite regularly, yet never go to church. Even those who no longer pray see some value in it. Typically, Barry Norman recently said in *The Sunday Times*, 'Until well into my twenties I used to pray at night.' Then he wistfully added, 'I don't now. Maybe I should.' But many, like Lord Althorpe, Princess Di's brother, still do. In fact, it's jokingly said that there are more people in our society who pray to God than believe he exists!

With prayer goes an emphasis on the value of faith. It's not faith in God or in anything particular – just faith in faith. The average nice Britisher will tell you, after an illness, 'It was my faith that got me through'. 'Faith' gives you 'the ability to face things'. It's a deep, fundamental belief that ultimately the world is not chaotic, that it does make sense, that there is an order to it and that good will finally triumph.

Alongside this faith is a fairly superstitious view of the world. Extraordinary measures are adopted to ensure good luck and avoid bad luck. Trivial, but numerous, irrational actions will be indulged in to ensure that fate can't do its worst to you. These range from the common actions of touching wood, not walking under ladders, throwing spilt salt over your left shoulder, not lighting a cigarette a third time, rejoicing when a black cat crosses your path and believing that a broken mirror will bring you seven years' bad luck, to much more serious superstitious beliefs. Some whole fishing communities, for example, are riddled with superstitions which say it is bad luck for the men to pass their women on the way to their boats, or which dictate when they should or should not put out to sea.

In addition to this there is a side to common religion which touches on the church. Many people will turn to the church at the great crisis points of life, those of birth, marriage and death. In the case of the former two, we complain that they do it just because the church is a pretty setting for the photographs. But perhaps it's a little deeper than that. Since people are made in God's image, however marred that image may be, is it really surprising that when confronted with the wonder of birth, the mystery of marriage or the threat of death they should want to turn to someone beyond for thanksgiving, prayer and help? At such moments the desire to reach out to some greater power is profound.

Even more, a large number of people whom we would never count as active Christians have some attachment to or involvement with an activity of the church such as the women's meeting, the Boys' Brigade or some other club or society. They may not belong, but they are in touch and have not dismissed religion completely.

Others go even further and do treat the church as theirs, whether they go or not! If the ecclesiastical authorities wish to close it down, they are the first to protest. If the new vicar wants to make changes, they are the first to oppose him. He is a religious professional, but also a religious outsider striving to impose a pure spirituality on their muddied religious culture, and they will not have it. Local and family traditions are more important than theological purity.

Church, especially in the older villages, is a community institution rather than a religious one. The great events in the church's calendar are not those of the major religious festivals but of the Sunday school anniversary, the chapel anniversary and the harvest supper – all social, rather than primarily religious, events.

Story after story proves the point. One harvest festival, an enthusiastic Methodist local preacher challenged his congregation as to whether they really would follow Jesus after they had sung 'Follow, follow, I will follow Jesus' during the offering. Apparently he went too far and was much criticized for it afterwards. As the researcher said, 'The serious concerns of religion should not be allowed to interfere with one's enjoyment of the Harvest Festival'.

From a Christian viewpoint one might want to dismiss all this as grossly inadequate if not dangerously misleading. It could be a stepping-stone to the real thing but is often a cheap and harmful substitute. Even so, it is an indication that the world is not as secular as many would suggest.

Religious interpretations are more commonly resorted to than the secularists would have us believe.

Perhaps a tiny indication of the widespread religious sensitivity that many still feel was seen when lightning struck York Minster early on a July morning in 1984, shortly after the enthronement of the controversial Bishop of Durham, causing extensive fire damage. While the religious professionals rushed to assure the press that this was not and could not be an act of God, for it was not the sort of thing he was capable of, thousands of ordinary people apparently had no difficulty in interpreting it in that light. It is difficult to proclaim the world as secular while such interpretations are widely given.

New religious movements

As we look around, there is other evidence, too, that the world is far from secular. In some respects the 1960s and 1970s reached the pinnacle of secular permissiveness. But not in all respects. Those same decades when media men and theologians alike were declaring that God was dead were decades of tremendous religious creativity. Hundreds of new religious movements were being brought to birth. They covered everything from Jonestown, where 913 followers of James Jones committed mass suicide in November 1978, to the Moonies, noted for their deceptive proselytizing tactics and mass weddings, the largest of which so far has been the marriage of 5,837 couples simultaneously in October 1982.

Some of these new religious movements are offshoots or perversions of orthodox Christianity. Some run counter to the dominant culture of the West and import oriental religious techniques such as those which the Beatles briefly popularized. Others are more introverted and opt for the development of inner human potential.

Statistically they may be small, but they are certainly not insignificant. It has been estimated that such movements have ninety-six million adherents world-wide. In the United States it has been calculated that 5% of the twenty-one to thirty-five age group have been directly exposed to a new religious movement of an oriental kind.

The fact remains that while traditional religions have been in decline the new religious movements have been growing. Many will not last. Yet they show that even if the traditional religious interpretation of the world has been rejected a religious perspective on the world is still enormously important to millions.

Many have in fact understood them as a reaction to the secular world which the 1960s and 1970s were creating. It was a barren and impersonal world where science dominated, regardless of personal feelings. In that situation the traditional churches lost confidence and sounded their trumpets in a very uncertain way. These new religions were different. They offered direct religious experience, an authoritative interpretation of life, a genuine sense of belonging and the offer of an alternative to mainstream secular society. Hence many found them attractive.

The occult

We could cast our gaze more widely. For a secular society there is an amazing amount of occult activity about.

Of course, not all those who participate in occult activities believe in them. They treat them like a harmless game, but it is the devil who puts about the lie that they are not to be taken for real.

What is interesting is just how much the occult is evident in a secular society. Maybe it is by way of reaction to the boredom of secularism, but who would have thought that witches would be interviewed so regularly on the television, Russell Grant's horoscopes would become a regular part of Breakfast Time television, witchcraft would be the major theme of a number of children's serials and that sales of magazines and books on the occult would soar into big business? Whether treated seriously or not, the existence of a spirit world and the reality of a dimension of evil seem to have gained widespread acceptance.

These 'soft' expressions of the occult are only the tip of

the iceberg. While it is very difficult to be dogmatic about the existence and extent of satanic organizations, it is clear that such groups exist. Various areas of our country are notorious for the presence of witches' covens devoted to the rituals of black magic. The artefacts of satanic rituals are discovered from time to time. Some have openly said that as satanists they are praying for the breakdown of family life and the destruction of many things which Christians hold sacred. Most recently the trial of Derry Manwaring, accused of obtaining thousands of pounds from rich evangelical Christians for use in bringing about the downfall of satanist groups, brought the existence of such groups to public attention. The trial began to expose a world which many would find hard to believe in. But there can be little doubt that he was not engaged in a clever fraud. Rather he was caught in the real, powerful but destructive world of the satanic.

The extraordinary way in which people commit themselves to new religious movements or occult practices is truly astonishing. It reminds me of a comment of Malcolm Muggeridge. He claims, 'One of the peculiar sins of the twentieth century which we have developed to a very high level is the sin of credulity. It has been said that when human beings stop believing in God they believe in nothing. The truth is much worse; they believe in anything.'

Reviewing the situation

Others would want to cast the net wider still and look at the way we live and act religiously in areas of our lives which do not apparently have much to do with religion. This is a more complex and controversial area and one which we need not enter to substantiate our argument. But some see sex, drugs, families, health or even work as new religions which have taken over where the old have left off.

It would seem that man is not as secular as at first sight he would appear. Scratching a little beneath the surface, we find that secular man is still quite religious underneath. It may be that just at the moment he is less religious than he was in the past. But that does not mean that his world will inevitably become more and more secular. There is already evidence that many are bored with their secular environment and there is also the widespread fear that technology may let us down on a massive scale. Technology is an unstable god to worship.

Does that mean, then, that the picture of our world as one without windows is invalid? No. It qualifies that picture in some important respects but does not invalidate it. The evidence that man is still religious means that the secularist should not be so glib about his pronouncements that God is dead. But it is still true that, for the moment, the secularist appears to have the upper hand.

What is interesting about the evidence of this chapter is that whether we are talking of folk religion, new religious movements or the occult, none of these are socially significant. They are private expressions of religion which have little effect on the public world where reality is defined. The academics who teach our children are sceptical about them. The politicians who make our laws largely ignore them. They will pay lip service to religion on state occasions and may ask questions in the House about some religious movements which are considered a social liability, but religion does not seriously affect their debates. The media treats them as one might an elderly grandfather, an interesting oddity but not to be taken too seriously. The public atmosphere we breathe is decidedly secular.

We must therefore consider how we are to live and survive in such an atmosphere. We must remember that what we are experiencing is only the latest form of a long-established virus. Since the situation is not novel, the Bible can give us some helpful guide-lines. Mercifully, it shows that whenever the virus has been on the rampage there have been pockets of resistance, antibodies, which have effectively countered it.

PART TWO

Looking at the Bible

4
What does the
Old Testament say?

At first sight the Old Testament is of little value in discussing secularization. Its people seem to live in a world where belief in the supernatural is easy and where gods abound. It is true that they may have argued over which god was superior, but nobody seems to have doubted their existence or their influence on man's affairs. A religious understanding of the world was for real.

But when we probe a little deeper, we begin to see that, in their own way, the people of the Old Testament struggled with the threat of secularism like everyone else. They faced the constant temptation to allow the temporal to exclude the eternal and to replace God with man and God's creation with a world of man's own making. The pull of secularism started early – as early as the Garden of Eden (Gen 3).

Secularism right from the start

The serpent caused Eve to question God's word. The first temptation that mankind meets is, interestingly enough, dressed up in the guise of a theological discussion! That in itself was not secularism. But it is important to note how the conversation is described in detail.

The serpent offers Eve the chance to have her eyes opened and become 'like God' (Gen 3:5). Eve gives in because 'she saw that the fruit of the tree was good for food and pleasing to the eye, and also desirable for gaining wisdom . . .' (6). So the desire for man to replace God with himself begins immediately after man is created. And that desire is assisted by the lure of the material through the visual senses and by the quest for knowledge.

From the beginning then, three elements of secularism were evident: the removal of God from his righful place, the temptation of the material and the thirst for knowledge independent of God. The rift that Eve's action brought about between God and man then rapidly developed and new forms of behaviour quickly reinforced it.

Cities, technology and land

An alternative security arrangement

The very next generation was responsible for building a city. Cain built it and named it after his son Enoch (Gen 4:17). Cain had murdered his brother and had been punished by God for doing so. His sentence was that he was to find working on the land a hard slog and that he was to be a fugitive all his life. Even so, God offered him protection. It would seem, however, that having left the presence of God, he no longer felt that he could trust God and so resorted to building a city for his own protection. Dissatisfied with God's security, he sought to manufacture his own in a city. The city becomes something of a symbol for secular man in the Old Testament and significantly remains the place, even today, where people find it least easy to believe in God.

An ambiguous symbol: are cities holy or hostile?

It is true that the symbolism of the city is not straight-forward in the Old Testament. It is not always a centre of hostility to God. God commands that cities of refuge be built (Num 35 and Josh 20). The city of Nineveh turns from its sin and turns to God (Jon 3). And Jerusalem occupies a special place as a holy city where the praises of God and the prosperity of the city are inextricably inter-twined (Ps 122). But, for the most part, the city is the man-built centre of resistance to God. It is the place which man builds for his own glory, where man seeks his own security. It is the centre from which war is waged and where sin is unrestrained. That can be seen in the early stories about the Tower of Babel (Gen 11:1–9) and Sodom (Gen 18:20–19:28). In Egypt, the use of Israelite slaves in the building of cities was the means of oppressing the people of God (Exod 1:11, 14).

Entering Canaan, it was cities like Jericho which stood in opposition to God's plans and needed to be destroyed (Josh 6:2–27). Under the monarchy, not only do we have the sneaking feeling that Solomon's motives are mixed – he beautified Jerusalem so that some of the glory went to God and some of the glory went to him (2 Chron 3:1–5:1; 6:1,2) – but we have the pitiful spectacle of Rehoboam. He lost ten tribes of his kingdom through his own foolishness (2 Chron 10:1–17) and then set about building cities in a pathetic attempt to preserve what little was left (2 Chron 11:5–12).

When the life of the nation had totally degenerated, the people of Israel were exiled from the land that God had given them and held captive in Babylon (2 Chron 36:15–20). This proud city with all its boasted power and eminence once more oppressed God's people and for ever after was held up as the symbol of organized opposition to God. When Peter and John wanted to write in the New Testament about cities of their own day which opposed God they readily used the code-name of Babylon for them, knowing that the interpretation would be immediately apparent to their readers (1 Pet 5:13; Rev 18).

Jerusalem does stand somewhat apart from these other cities and yet is not wholly distinct from them. It is true that it was the centre of the worship of Yahweh and that when the prophets wish to portray a future of hope they do so by describing a restored Jerusalem (Isa 44:24–28; Mal 3:4). Through David's covenant with God she becomes his special city (2 Sam 5:9), a light to the nations and the means of judgment on others. Yet Jerusalem was also the city where sin was committed (Jer 13:27; Mic 1:5) and where God's messengers, the prophets, were rejected (2 Chron 36:16; Matt 23:37). The covenant does not exempt her from succumbing to the special temptations to which the city is prone.

The spiritual nature of the city

The Bible's perspective on the city would seem to suggest that the city is not just a sociological phenomenon but a spiritual one. It seems that from this standpoint the city generates a spiritual power which causes man to be proud, sinful and independent of God. God's condemnation of Tyre sums it up:

> In the pride of your heart you say, 'I am a god; I sit on the throne of a god in the heart of the seas.' But you are a man and not a god, though you think you are as wise as a god . . . Because you think you are wise, as wise as a god, I am going to bring foreigners against you, the most ruthless of nations; they will draw their swords against your beauty and wisdom and pierce your shining splendour . . . Will you then say, 'I am a god,' in the presence of those who kill you? (Ezek 28:2–9)

It is perhaps the outworking of this judgment in our own day which, among other things, must be taken into account in trying to cope with the seemingly intractable problems of our cities.

Technology – its double-edged nature

Within seven generations from Adam the beginnings of technology had already taken place. We read that Tubal-Cain 'forged all kinds of tools out of bronze and iron' (Gen 4:22). The shepherd and the artist had now been joined by the primitive technologist. In itself technology may be spiritually neutral. It may be the outworking of God's commission to man to subdue the earth (Gen 1:28). Where this is so, humanity benefits as advances are made which improve the quality of life and ease its hardships. Who would want to give up many of the splendid technological achievements that make life so good? But technology, alas, is not always used in that way. Man not only makes tools, he also makes weapons. As much as he improves life by technology, he also destroys life by the same technology. So it was in the Old Testament. Tubal-Cain made tools, but it was not long before the same skills were fashioning instruments of violence and destruction, and military technology became dominant (Judg 1:19). Whether the use made of technology was good or evil, it often stood over against God as an alternative object in which man could put his faith. Psalm 20:7 sums up the choice neatly: 'Some trust in chariots and some in horses, but we trust in the name of the Lord our God.' The threat that technology could become an alternative god has been with us ever since, and is a powerful factor enticing us in the direction of secularization.

It would be unwise to conclude from this that all good Christians who wish to avoid secularism should leave the cities, turn their back on technological achievement, go and live in the country and engage only in cottage industry. The urban environment may be spiritually more hostile than the rural environment, but the issue must not be treated simplistically.

The Old Testament makes it clear that the countryside

can also be a tempting place. On the face of it rural life seems to be more favourable to a religious perspective. It does not envelop people in a man-made environment. Rather it keeps them closer to the miracle of life and nature and the coming and going of the seasons. The farmer is dependent on forces beyond his control in a way in which the factory worker is not. So he has a flying start when it comes to matters of a spiritual kind. Even so, nature itself may become the object of worship. The desire for abundant crops may lead to the rural community worshipping at the shrine of a fertility goddess rather than at the shrine of the living God. And when nature fails grumbling grows and that easily transforms itself, through bitterness, into unbelief. Nowadays, the 'agricultural industry' is much more dependent on technology and this makes the differences between the urban and rural environments, together with their spiritual implications, less significant than they were.

The land: gift and responsibility

The basic principle which underlies all Old Testament teaching in this regard is that land belongs to the Lord: 'To the Lord your God belong the heavens . . . the earth and everything in it' (Deut 10:14); 'The earth is the Lord's, and everything in it . . .' (Ps 24:1). Even so, he has given it as a gift to man, who is now responsible for it. So without any contradiction, Psalm 115:16 can voice another perspective: 'The highest heavens belong to the Lord, but the earth he has given to man.'

Man's attitude to the land, therefore, needs to be kept in fine balance. On the one hand, land is a gift which God has *given* to man. So it is perfectly legitimate for man to appear to possess the land and even dwell in privately owned property. The Bible never criticizes private ownership in principle, although it is frequently critical of it in practice. The gift also means that God has made man responsible for it. So man dare not neglect it but should manage it to the full extent that wisdom will allow. On the other hand, land is *never more than a gift* and ultimately remains the property of God. So man dare not be arrogant, believing that he has any right to it. Nor dare he exploit it selfishly or possess it greedily, as if he owns it, no matter who suffers. God has given it to others too.

The trouble is that this is just what man does forget. He easily falls into the trap of believing that he has a right to it; he has earned it, the world owes it to him, and his family and generation are the only ones who matter. Humility goes out of the window with wisdom and they are replaced by arrogance and selfish exploitation. It was because of this tendency that God warned the children of Israel when they settled in the promised land:

> When the Lord your God brings you into the land he swore to your fathers, to Abraham, Isaac and Jacob, to give you – a land with large, flourishing cities you did not build, houses filled with all kinds of good things you did not provide, wells you did not dig, and vineyards and olive groves you did not plant – then when you eat and are satisfied, be careful that you do not forget the Lord, who brought you out of Egypt, out of the land of slavery. (Deut 6:10–12)

> For the Lord your God is bringing you into a good land . . . When you have eaten and are satisfied, praise the Lord your God for the good land he has given you. Be careful that you do not forget the Lord your God, failing to observe his commands, his laws and his decrees . . . (Deut 8:7–11)

Desire and 'the possessions trap'

The desire to possess and to treat property as if it is one's own is not limited to land. Desire is so endemic to man that God outlawed covetousness in the ten commandments (Exod 20:17). By doing so, he showed how seriously he treated the matter and, to some extent, exercised restraint over it.

But desire is not so easily dealt with, as the story of Achan shows. When the children of Israel conquered Jericho they were forbidden to take as loot any of the gold, silver, bronze and iron since such things were to be devoted to the Lord alone (Josh 6:18,19). But Achan could not resist the temptation and took some forbidden goods and hid them in his tent with the tragic result that he brought destruction on his family and judgment on the whole of Israel (Josh 7). There is an Achan in all of us.

The connection between covetousness and secularism is twofold. Firstly, the desire to have something within our possession is a desire to displace God. In his desire man seeks to act as the owner and ruler of the world and its resources, a role that rightly belongs to God alone. But secondly, and paradoxically, in attempting to control material things man finds that he ends up being controlled by them himself. In the words of Paul's stinging exposure of society, man 'worshipped and served created things rather than the Creator' (Rom 1:25). The correct attitude towards material possessions is to be found in 1 Timothy 4:4, 5: 'For everything God created is good, and nothing is to be rejected if it is received with thanksgiving, because it is consecrated by the word of God and prayer.' Without thanksgiving, man's thinking quickly becomes horizontal, his environment becomes materialistic and God is pushed beyond his horizons.

Idolatry and pluralism

Idols: do-it-yourself deities

All this is closely connected with another theme which frequently crops up in the Old Testament, that of idolatry. An idol is simply a man-made object of worship which displaces the true and living God. It is simply ridiculous, as prophets like Isaiah (Isa 44:6–22) and Jeremiah (Jer 10:1–16) kept pointing out, that man should bow down and worship what he himself has made; objects which are far more impotent and less gifted than man himself is. Even so, man keeps making and submitting to idols.

The ancient world was well populated with idols and it did not take Israel long to learn the art of idol-making, so adding to the population explosion among tin gods. After they had been delivered from Egypt, the children of Israel became impatient at the long absence of Moses who was away consulting the Lord, and decided to make their own deity (Exod 32). Worshipping the invisible is difficult in a material world. So they melted down their jewellery and used tools to create a golden calf.

The absurd irrationality of man is then seen in Aaron's claim that, 'These are your gods, O Israel, who brought you up out of Egypt' (Exod 32:4). How can something just made by man be said to have delivered man previously from Egypt? The incident initiates Israel's on-off love affair with idolatry which persisted for centuries.

Priorities in worship

Idolatry is ultimately man worshipping himself. It leaves no room for the living God. True worship is radically different from it and there is no room for compromise between the two.

God knows how subtle the temptation is for man to intrude himself in worship. That is why he demands that when the children of Israel erect a stone altar they should 'not build it with dressed stones, for you will defile it if you use a tool on it' (Exod 20:25). Man's desire to improve on God's command is usually the first step down the slippery slope that leads away from God. Dressing the stones may have originally been the expression of a genuine desire to make the altar the best that it could be for God. But before long, dressing the stones would have become an end in itself and the worship of God would have become a secondary activity until it was eventually squeezed out altogether. One can just imagine the formation of stone-dressers' guilds and stone-dressing anniversaries, and all the paraphernalia which go with such things and which so often

cause us to mistake the means with the end itself. So God
will have none of it.

Encountering pluralism

The mention of idolatry reminds us, too, that the Old
Testament world was a pluralist world. We often speak of
pluralism as if it were a modern discovery but it is not. We
may be more conscious of it now because of the media and
increased mobility. But the Old Testament peoples were
also mobile, either voluntarily or because of political
upheavals, and knew what it was to encounter at close
quarters religious cultures which were very different from
their own.

A chequered history

On entering Canaan they were confronted by religions
which many found to have more appeal than their own
because they were more sensuous and material. God's
approach to pluralism at the time was to impose a rigid
policy of purity and separation on them (see, for example,
Deut 13; 16:21; 18:9–13 and Joshua). It was essential if
true worship was to survive. Israel simply could not have
coexisted with other nations and survived.

Subsequent history shows how, for all the safeguards,
many in Israel did not remain true to God. The pluralistic
atmosphere in which they lived led many to worship unauthorized gods in unauthorized ways at unauthorized high
places. The crunch came when Elijah challenged the
prophets of Baal, the name for local gods in Canaan, to a
show-down on Mount Carmel. Despite their popular
following, they were humiliatingly defeated and the power
of the living God was convincingly demonstrated (1 Kings
18:16–46).

Even so, Israel did not learn. Compromise with other
gods soon developed again, and in spite of another clean-
up campaign, inspired by Josiah (2 Chron 34), the trend
was unmistakably downhill as far as spiritual reality was
concerned.

The frightening implications
Israel's spiritual adultery eventually led God to punish them by almost totally destroying their land and their culture and subjecting them to exile in Babylon. That in itself led to a new phase in the history of pluralism.

Israel was no longer the host nation tempted to indulge tolerantly the religions of others. She was now a subject people, overawed by others. The gods of the Babylonians seemed to have won the day and have the upper hand. A crisis of faith therefore arose. They could no longer see God in their affairs. Where was he? Was their own God no longer able to cope? Were the claims which had been made for him, claims that made him the supreme controller of history, false? Had he been defeated? And even if you still believed, how could you remain faithful to God in a foreign land where the laws did not favour you or the practice of your religion? We shall explore this more fully in chapter eight, but for the moment we simply want to note that the experience of pluralism is one which was known in the Old Testament. We might therefore gain some insight from its teaching into how we should cope with it today.

Politics and economics

Politics: who's to be in charge?
Perhaps the clearest secularizing factor in the Old Testament is one which we have yet to mention. God intended that the people of Israel should be a theocracy, that is to say that God himself would be their king. Human agents of government, which would be necessary, would be of a very limited nature and would rule in strict accordance with God's law. His plan was that they should be different from all other nations on earth (Exod 33:15, 16). But they were not happy with the arrangement and wanted to be just the same as everyone else so that they could look to men for their security and protection. This chiefly expressed itself politically. God did not want them to have a king and

warned them that they would be exploited if they did (1 Sam 8:7–18). But they insisted, 'We want a king over us. Then we shall be like all the other nations, with a king to lead us and to go out before us and fight our battles' (1 Sam 8:19, 20). The king was given, and God's predictions came true.

Again the situation is not unambiguous. David proved a great king, close to the heart of God, and a great warrior too. But, on balance, kings proved spiritually disastrous and behaved just like all the other despotic kings of the earth. They went to battle for their own glory rather than at God's command. They built buildings for their own prestige rather than God's glory. They governed without consulting God sufficiently. And ironically, in spite of using people to their own ends, they displaced God as the object of the people's trust.

Economics: riches – but at whose expense?

What was true in the political sphere was equally true economically. Secularizing forces led the people away from obeying God's economic plan for them and towards following their own.

The book of Leviticus reveals God's carefully worked out economic system which was designed to prevent the rich from getting richer and the poor from getting poorer. The law was there to eliminate the poverty trap and to ensure that Israel was a humane, compassionate and socially just society. That was the clear objective of legislation such as that found buried in Leviticus 19, or the more obvious teaching regarding the Sabbath and the year of Jubilee in Leviticus 25. But Israel chose to be like other nations and to live according to so-called economic realities instead of God's word. So a wedge was driven between spiritual truth and economic practice, the result of which was that Israel became anything but a compassionate society. Social divisions multiplied as the rich got richer and the poor had no means of survival.

There is no clearer expression of this than in the book

of Amos. Money was supreme (Amos 3:10,15; 6:4–6), the poor were exploited (2:7; 4:1; 5:11) and justice was perverted (2:7; 5:7,10; 8:4–6). God had therefore withdrawn from them (8:11) and judgment was on its way (3:11–4:3). What God wanted was simple: 'Hate evil, love good; maintain justice in the courts' (5:15); 'But let justice roll on like a river, righteousness like a never-failing stream!' (5:24). If they repented and returned to God, then he would have mercy on them.

Any approach to politics or economics which tries to place them in a separate compartment from religion is bound to have the same devastating effect. Secularism says that man should stand on his own feet and cope with the realities of life without reference to God. But God is the biggest reality in life and any attempt to exclude him can only lead to the same disastrous consequences.

Chasing the wind

From a different perspective the book of Ecclesiastes provides us with an autopsy on secularism. Scholars dispute whether it is written by a cynic or whether the author is using a clever device to reveal the emptiness of the secular life. Either way, it concerns the philosophy of life lived 'under the sun', life which is lived on the horizontal level alone and which has blotted out the existence of God. If God is ignored then there is no meaning and no pleasure to be found in anything. 'Meaningless futility' is the only verdict which can sensibly be written over man's existence.

The quest for meaning

The author has certainly not reached this conclusion lightly. Much of the book consists of his confession as to how he tried to find meaning and significance. He details a shopping list of ways by which meaningfulness can be purchased. Wisdom (Eccl 1:12–18), pleasure (2:1–11), work (2:17–23), power (4:1–16), and money (5:8–20) – he's tried them all and found them dead ends. Why bother with wisdom when fools seem to prosper just as much? Pleasure never seems to reward its seeker with satisfaction but condemns him rather to a never-ending quest. And where does work get you in the end, except a lot of trouble? Power goes hand in hand with corruption and injustice. And money? Well, when you've got it you have to leave it all to someone else.

Is there any point?
Living under the sun is like chasing the wind. You keep trying but you never win. Life is a repetitive bore. It makes no sense. You want to argue with it but it won't argue back. It doesn't give. It doesn't negotiate. You live it, and no matter how you live it your destiny is the same as everyone else's. Death is the great leveller. Wise and foolish, men about town and solid squares, captains of industry and those in the dole queue, powerful and oppressed, rich and poor – it ultimately doesn't matter because death comes to all and renders everything even more meaningless. If the world is a closed system, that's it.

Life from a different point of view
But what if there is life above the sun as well? If there is a God, the whole picture changes. From time to time, as the writer of Ecclesiastes pours out his depressing tale, he cannot help but inject a brief comment about God. God is the creator who has set eternity in man's hearts (Eccl 3:11). So it is not surprising if there is no meaning apart from him. Trying to understand life apart from God is like trying to solve one of those annoying puzzles you get as stocking-fillers at Christmas. Unless you have the vital piece in place the rest makes no sense whatsoever.

If God be God then he will be so great that we cannot possibly understand him, and true wisdom begins with recognizing our limitations (3:11; 11:5). We must accept our creatureliness and approach his majestic holiness with reverence (3:14; 5:2). Yet this awesome God is the one who

gives men the gift of satisfaction (3:13; 5:19). He also gives
men hope that justice will one day be done and sense will
one day be revealed (3:15, 17; 11:9). Belief may not provide
us with all the answers. But it makes much greater sense
than unbelief. The first answer to the enigma of life, therefore, is to fear God (12:13). All else follows from that.
Secularism is bankrupt because it simply does not make
sense of our existence. In showing the emptiness of the
secular philosophy, Ecclesiastes still speaks powerfully to
our own day.

Summary

The Old Testament has plenty of points of identity with
our own day in its struggle against secularism. They built
their proud man-made cities and we live in a predominantly
urban environment. They developed technology and we are
basically technological in approach. That led them, as us,
to the temptations of materialism and the worship of man-
made gods. Like us, they were surrounded by people who
adopted other world-views whose presence threatened to
undermine their own world-view. They too divorced the
public world of politics and economics, the 'real' world,
from the world of religion. Their philosophical speculation
led some to unbelieving scepticism as much philosophical
enquiry does today. The form in which we encounter secularizing tendencies seems to us distinctly modern. But the
themes are as old as mankind itself.

In grappling with the issues the Old Testament reveals
principles which need to be carefully reinterpreted for our
own day. But above all, it provides us with a radical critique
of secularism. It surely provides us with ample evidence to
suggest that man's attempt to live without the true and
living God can only be disastrous. A secular world is not
only a boring world but a bad world.

5
What does the New Testament say?

There is an old Peanuts cartoon where Charlie Brown is studying a book very intently and at very close quarters. Lucy asks him what he is doing and he says he's reading between the lines. When we come to ask what the New Testament says about secularism we have to do a little reading between the lines. Secularism is not obvious. Indeed, since the culture of the time lacked one of the most powerful ingredients of secularism, a scientific framework, it would be surprising if people had been highly secular in their thinking.

In spite of that disclaimer, however, people still found it difficult to believe in an invisible God. You only have to read the letter to the Hebrews to see that. Man's submission to the authority of his own mind peeps through the pages of the New Testament. In the background of the New Testament, pluralism is rife. And 'the world' too easily hogs the centre of the stage, even for Christians. Add to this the radical critique that the New Testament provides of fallen man's mind and we certainly have quite a few pointers as to how we should be living in a secular world.

Earthly thinking

One verse neatly summarizes the pull of secularism which can be found in the days of the New Testament. In 1 Corinthians 1:22 Paul wrote, 'Jews demand miraculous signs and Greeks look for wisdom . . .'

Not enough evidence

Let's begin with the Jews. They may have had little problem believing in God, but the seeds of secularism are evident in their approach to Jesus. They believed that when the Messiah came they would be able to recognize him by the miraculous works he performed. John accepts the validity of this approach and so, in his Gospel, sets out to provide the evidence that they were seeking, in order that the Jews might come to believe that Jesus is the Christ, the Son of God (John 20:31). He argues that the faith of the Christian is well-grounded. It is not an irrational leap into the absurd. Faith does not demand a mindless commitment to nonsense.

So from the beginning of his Gospel (John 2:11) he shows how the true nature of Jesus was revealed through miraculous signs and that these led to faith in him. For John, seeing is an important ingredient of believing. We have therefore dubbed Thomas the patron saint of doubters with less than total justice (John 20:25). It is more likely that, from John's viewpoint, Thomas was legitimately asking for evidence before believing in the resurrection.

But God's graciousness in providing evidence entails a risk. And this is where the seeds of secularism can germinate and grow. The minds of fallen human beings too easily become arrogant. They fail to accept the evidence and demand more and more before they will be satisfied. That was what happened to the Jews among whom Jesus lived. They were never satisfied and never would be, no matter how many miracles he performed. They stood aloof in their non-commitment, making their own minds the final arbiter instead of God's revelation. Signs are not mechanical proof.

They only ever provide supportive evidence which still leaves room for faith. But the secular mind cannot interpret the signs in a way which will lead it to the living God. Paul makes the same point in 1 Corinthians 2:14.

The minds of fallen human beings are warped. They see the signs and are content to stop with them rather than going beyond them to the reality they signify. It is like going on a journey from London to Edinburgh. As you travel up the A1 you eventually see the name of Edinburgh on a sign-post. Who in their right mind would stop there thinking that they had arrived at the city itself? The sign-post simply points you in the right direction. Yet time and again the Jews wanted signs and were not prepared to go beyond to the reality of which they spoke. Jesus rebuked them for it (see, for example, John 4:48; 6:26–30) but it made little difference. Their quest for primitive scientific evidence to support the view that Jesus was the Messiah verged on the borders of grotesque sensation-seeking and curiosity-mongering. It was very earthly thinking. It would certainly not get them to heaven.

Within the general context of the Jews demanding proof there were some men who were particularly down-to-earth in their thinking and would have taken a lot of persuading before they would believe anything out-of-the-ordinary at all: the Sadducees. These were a group of priests and laymen who formed the elite of Jewish society. They were a rich, conservative aristocracy who had much invested in their world and a lot to lose if anything disturbed the status quo. Believers in God and champions of the Old Testament law, they argued that the law should be interpreted simply and literally. In this regard they were unlike the Pharisees whom they accused of importing novelties into their Old Testament interpretation.

The Sadducees had a strong belief in free will and consequently rejected any notion of predestination or of God taking the initiative. They are well known to readers of the New Testament for their dismissal of the idea of resurrection (Mark 12:18) and of any belief in angels or demons

(Acts 23:8). In rejecting these things they effectively removed God from having any real power of intervention in his world.

Theirs was a this-wordly religion which, it has been said, had doctrinal views which 'were tempered by the "common sense" of contemporary secular thought'. They were not pure secularists, because they did believe in God. But they were in danger of becoming secularists. John Wimber, the well-known American evangelist and teacher, has said: 'The assumption of secular minds is that we live in a universe closed off from divine intervention, in which truth is arrived at through empirical means and rational thought.' They were well on the road to just those assumptions.

Not enough philosophy

We turn our attention now to the Greeks. The classical age of the great philosophers had passed and Greek philosophy was more favourable to religion than once it had been. But their great love was speculative thought and abstract argument. Philosophy was the final arbiter of truth, in so far as truth was a meaningful concept. Many of the ideas which lay at the heart of the Christian faith were completely rejected as philosophically unacceptable. That God should have become incarnate in flesh was unacceptable, since flesh to them was evil. That God should suffer, as Christians claimed Christ did, was unacceptable, for God was impassive. That there should be a resurrection of the body was unacceptable, as Paul found out in Athens (Acts 17:32), even though they believed in the immortality of the soul.

There may be only the occasional explicit reference to the Greeks in the New Testament, such as when Paul speaks at Mars Hill or writes his opening words to the Corinthians, but their assumptions quickly infiltrated the church and adulterated its purity. Several of the New Testament letters are therefore written to combat the insidious influence Greek philosophy had on the early Christians. They were not total secularists, as they did not believe in a closed universe. But their exaltation of human reasoning sowed seeds from which secularism could blossom centuries later.

There were others, with no particularly well-worked-out philosophy, who were sceptics. There are always plenty of people who do not know what they believe themselves but are prepared to undermine the faith of others by pouring ridicule on it. New Testament Christians certainly encountered such people, especially when they spoke about their faith in the Lord's return (Jude 18 and 2 Pet 3:3,4).

Meeting the challenge of earthly thinking

How did the early Christians cope with the encroachment of these secularist ideas? Two aspects of their reaction are evident.

Firstly *they refused to compromise*. They did not negotiate with those who did not believe in a resurrection of the body, whether they were godly Sadducees or philosophical Greeks. Their belief was asserted and the ground was firmly held. Every secularist tendency was carefully examined and refuted.

But secondly, and more positively, *they tried to persuade others of the correctness of their position*. John's Gospel is an example of a detailed argument aimed at convincing unbelieving Jews to put their faith in Jesus. Similarly, Paul's approach was to argue the faith and use every honest means at his disposal to persuade unbelievers of the logic and sense of his position (eg Acts 17:4; 18:4; 2 Cor 5:11).

57 varieties of religion

We forget that Jesus was not exceptional in founding a new religion. His world was full of religions, ancient and modern, and someone was always trying to add another to the existing variety. Jesus, of course, lived and taught in a Jewish context where there was a large amount of consensus about religion. But even there they were exposed, through the infiltration of Greek ideas and by the presence of the occupying Roman army, to other religions.

A world teeming with gods

Once the Christian mission was propelled into a new orbit which took it beyond Palestine, the missionaries were projected into a universe which was well populated with gods. Paul and Barnabas were once mistaken for Greek gods (Acts 14:8–20) and Paul, like us today, had to grapple with a thoroughly pluralistic audience when he preached on Mars Hill (Acts 17:22–34). They were so concerned, in fact, not to neglect any god that the Greeks had even erected an altar to an unknown god. That altar, incidentally, reminds one of the comment of the English philosopher, Professor Alasdair MacIntyre: 'The creed of the English is that there is no God and that it is wise to pray to him from time to time.' Religion has always been approached as if it were an insurance policy.

Greek religion was based on the worship of the gods and goddesses of Mount Olympus. There were a plethora of deities and most city states had a patron god of their own. How seriously people believed in such gods is impossible to tell. Whatever the 'orthodox' view, at a popular level magic and superstition were rife.

Borrowed religions

Roman religion largely borrowed from Greek religion. But, after the time of Augustus, it contributed one new feature to the religious scene, the cult of emperor-worship. The person who took religion seriously might also belong to a mystery cult or society which would have its own initiation ceremonies, secret meals and private god, together with high ethical ideals. But for the most part, as long as one was a good citizen and observed civic duties without ruffling anyone's feathers, it did not really matter what you believed, or even how you behaved. The most common approach was syncretistic, that is, an approach which borrowed from one religion to another and happily mixed them all without worrying too much about their distinctiveness.

So Christianity did not develop in a highly Christianized

culture! It was one faith, and a weak one at that, offering a competing product in an overcrowded market-place which was already full of vigorous salesmen. It that respect it was much like our own day. Civic religion may have been more significant than it is now, but pluralism was none the less rampant.

Man at the top

Less recognizable as a religion was the worship of self. But it was a religion all the same, even if it lacked formal structures and systematic doctrines. We read of it in 2 Timothy 3:1–5 where Paul describes the worship of people in 'the last days'.

This religion is built on the twin foundations of self and materialism, according to verse 2. It essentially replaces the worship of God by the worship of man himself. Man ceases to be other-directed, and even less God-directed, and is motivated instead by what appears to fulfil his own self-centred needs and desires.

It is subjective and introverted. Man, having rejected God, has an aching void which he seeks desperately to fill by pampering himself in any way he feels might help. But such a religion has profound effects on the personalities of its adherents ('boastful, proud, abusive, disobedient'); on their families ('disobedient to their parents, ungrateful, unholy, without love, unforgiving, slanderous, without self-control'); and on society in general ('brutal, not lovers of the good, treacherous, rash, conceited, lovers of pleasure rather than lovers of God').

This religion is one of the most extreme forms of secularism because it dethrones God and enthrones man. The replacement of God at the centre by man at the centre is in part what sociologists mean by secularization. The transcendent and eternal are replaced by the introverted and immediate. Religious beliefs and practices are transformed into secular ones. The sacred is translated into the secular.

It is one of the most insidious forms of religion and must

be taken into account in trying to understand the mosaic of pluralism. False religions which have long traditions, sacred writings and clearer boundaries are easier to spot and deal with. But we might combat all of them yet still have the rug pulled from underneath our feet by the religion of 'selfism'.

Resisting the challenge

The response of the early Christians towards this pluralistic situation was one of 'no compromise'. But let's be careful to understand what they meant by that. 'No compromise' did not mean imposing their Christian patterns of behaviour on others through legislation. They were simply not in a position to do so, even if they had wanted to. Nor did it mean a censorious attitude to those who lived and believed differently. Their whole teaching led them to oppose prejudice, to demonstrate love and to live at peace with all men, whatever their religious background.

The 'no compromise' concerned the exclusiveness of the claims they made for their faith and the high moral standards they expected from their members. 'Salvation is found in no-one else, for there is no other name under heaven given to men by which we must be saved' (Acts 4:12).

Though sensitive to the cultural context in which they preached, and happy to adapt the language they used when appropriate, it was foreign to the early believers' thinking to negotiate with other religions in order to discover common reference points. They were not concerned to accommodate their beliefs to others. They had no hesitation in saying that Jesus was not '*a* way' but '*the* way'. He was the fulfilment of Judaism and, equally, what the Greeks in their philosophy and worship of the unknown God, had been seeking. But Jesus did not take his place on Mount Olympus as one of the pantheon.

The early disciples would have found our contemporary desire for dialogue strange. A letter from a Christian to *The Times* recently quoted an article from the *Journal of*

Ecumenical Studies with approval. It said:

> Dialogue and conversion are mutually exclusive . . . each participant in a sincere dialogue should confirm the other in his or her specific existence. Each becomes aware of the elements which unite them, accepting honestly those components of their faith which divide them and which each respects. No partners in dialogue should try to persuade the others of the exclusive truth of their own position.

If this is the currently accepted wisdom among missionaries, then the early Christians must surely feel that we have sold our heritage for a mess of pottage.

Worldliness

A simplistic solution

Secularization is not only to be found in the world, it is to be found in the church. Worldliness used to be easy. A few labels were stuck on the pub, cinema, and dance hall, forbidding Christians entry. A few practices like swearing, smoking, drinking and dancing were banned, and the problem was solved. Avoid them and holiness would grow. Only it didn't. Christians remained worldly, for all their taboos, because they had misinterpreted, or at best only partially interpreted, the New Testament teaching on the matter. Whenever the church adopts the spirit of the world, it is worldly. And that spells the secularization of the church.

What is worldliness, then?

The church is worldly when it lacks trust in God's control of the future and exhibits anxiety. It is worldly when it is ungrateful. It is worldly when its fellowship is full of gossip and backbiting. These are as much evidences of worldliness as are drunkenness or sexual immorality.

But there is one particular example of worldliness which has specific relevance for secularization. It is found in 1 John 2:15–17. John writes in stark terms that to be friendly to the world is to make oneself an enemy of God. By the world he means, 'the cravings of sinful man, the lust of his eyes and the boasting of what he has and does' (16). Significantly, these three features are very similar to those spelt out in the case of Eve's temptation in Genesis 3:6.

'The cravings of sinful man' speaks of temptation from within. Our fallen sinful natures constantly generate desires for sensual gratification. The older versions called it 'the desires of the flesh', because so much has to do with our physical and sexual drives.

'The lust of his eyes' recognizes that so much temptation finds its origin, or at least its encouragement, in what we see. Pornography is an obvious example. But being enticed by outward pomp and show is just as relevant. For all of us, the visual stimulus is a major factor in moving us towards sin. Here is temptation from without.

'The boasting of what he has and does' is 'hubris'. It is man's arrogant pride in himself and his possessions. It is a pride that is often without any foundation because we have achieved so little. And even if we have possessions to boast of, they are often possessions which really belong to the hire purchase company. John has in mind the way in which we constantly try to impress others with our non-existent importance. We invest so much significance in status and material possessions which really are of no significance. We live in an unceasing Vanity Fair. One of John DeLorean's friends remarked that his trouble was not his incompetence but simply hubris. That was what led to his downfall and will lead to the downfall of many others.

The inroads of secularization can be seen in these temptations. The material crowds out the spiritual, the visual excludes the unseen and this world expels the eternal from our consciousness. The answer of the early church in this area too was, once more, 'no compromise'.

Indictment of secular society

The 'no compromise' conclusion which the early Christians repeatedly reached sounds as if they were fighting a defensive rearguard action. In fact, they also took the offensive as Paul's graphic charge against fallen man shows.

In two passages, Romans 1:18–32 and Ephesians 4:17–19, Paul sets out the case against man cut adrift from God. Although it is clear that Paul has Gentiles in his gun sights in Ephesians, it is equally clear that the Jews are also in view in Romans. It is not a polemic of one man against others, or of one race against others, but a universal accusation against all men outside Christ.

It is sometimes difficult to think of our nice, respectable neighbours in these terms. But Paul wishes to jolt us into reality and to demonstrate the radical difference between the Christian and the non-Christian. The difference is not simply that one goes to church while the other does not. It is a total difference of mind-set and of life-principle.

Man without God (Romans)

The sentence: God's wrath
Romans 1:18 begins with the judge's sentence and only subsequently sets out the charge, evidence and verdict. The sentence is that the 'wrath of God is being revealed from heaven against all the godlessness and wickedness of men . . .' That may mean that the principle of God's judgment is already working itself out in individual lives and in society generally. It might equally mean that God's judgment has been shown to the world through the death of Christ. Either way, here is no uncontrolled anger or dispassionate, inevitable consequence of man's sin, but God's righteous, holy, loving, terrifying judgment on secular man.

The charge: ignoring the evidence
The sentence is justified because man is without excuse (19,

20). God has provided men with ample clues and sufficient grounds for believing in him. Creation itself does so. The problem lay not in the lack of evidence but in man's wilful rejection of the evidence he had. He knew God, but chose not to cultivate the relationship (21) and did not wish to 'retain the knowledge of God' (28).

A tragic sequence of consequences unfolds from that refusal. Because God was not worshipped, their capacity to think was reduced to futility and their personalities were imprisoned in darkness (21). Without God at the centre it is impossible to make real sense of the world or of life.

Ironically man does not understand his situation. He thinks he is living in the brilliant light of electricity, whereas he is existing in dim candle-light and he does not even realize it. No one has expressed it more clearly than Martin Luther in his *Bondage of the Will:*

> Scripture sets before us a man who is not only bound, wretched, captive, sick and dead, but who, through the operation of Satan, his Lord, adds to his other miseries that of blindness, so that he believes himself to be free, happy, possessed of liberty and ability, whole and alive.

The result: society in chaos

The great refusal brings in its train a great reversal. Wisdom is exchanged for folly (22), a living God for dead idols (23), clean living for immorality (24), truth for lies (25) and a Creator for things created (25).

God's part in this is to confirm men in the way they want to go. 'God gave them over' (26, 28) was the awful divine reaction. So man finds out just what sort of society his actions will create and what sort of persons it will breed (26–32). An uglier, more unlovely society could not be imagined. Yet sadly, we do not have to imagine it, for it is just the society in which we live. But rather than being brought to their senses and caused to return to God, men stubbornly persist in their secular ways.

Man rejecting God (Ephesians)

Much the same is said by Paul when he writes to the Ephesians.

Hardened hearts

Again he stresses that obstinacy lies at the root of man's problems. It is the 'hardening of their hearts' against God (Eph 4:18) that triggers a chain reaction of horrific proportions (18, 19). Obstinacy leads to ignorance. Man cannot learn of God unless he is willing to do so. Ignorance in turn leads to darkness and alienation from God.

Without that basic openness to God and knowledge of him, man is sentencing himself to grope around in folly, thinking that he is living in the light. What is more, he is a stranger to the one who made him and therefore it is impossible for him to live life to the full. Alienation from God renders man homeless in God's world. All that, in turn, leads man to live in destructive immorality, governed only by the thirst of his own passions which he is always seeking to assuage but which he never manages to quench.

Warped minds

Paul's emphasis in these verses is that there is a close connection between man's mind and man's behaviour. As a result of his rejection of God, man's mind is warped and inevitably, therefore, so is his behaviour. His perception of himself, his powers of reasoning, his intelligence, his mind, will and emotions are all damaged. Yet man lives and reasons as if they were perfectly reliable. Paul stresses that the damage is so severe that they are beyond repair. The only hope is not for renovation but for renewal (23,24). That is what makes the Christian so vitally different from the non-Christian.

These verses do not simply give us a transparent picture of our own society, they help us to unmask what lies behind it. It is not sufficient to denounce the evils we see around us. We must go deeper and expose the faulty thinking which causes them. And we must point out that man will never be able to reason aright while he thinks in a secular fashion. The root cause of all our difficulties is man's desire to think for himself, without reference to God.

A word of warning

Care must be taken not to misapply the survey sketched out in this chapter.

'No compromise' does not mean we must reject the world

The resilient 'no compromise' attitude of the early church, combined with the damning indictment given of man, sounds as if the only option for the Christian is to be totally negative about the world in which we live. Many have read it that way and have lived in their insulated Christian ghettos, happily letting the world go on its merry way to destruction. They have felt no responsibility for it socially or politically, and their spiritual concern has often only motivated them sufficiently to engage in a hit-and-run type of evangelism. But we must remember that it is secularism, the 'world' in the sense of society organized against God, which is being rejected and shunned, not the world which God loves.

God loves the world – and cares for it

The 'world' has other meanings in the New Testament. It is the place God created and the people whom he loved (John 3:16). His followers therefore cannot simply reject it. They of all people should be most able to enjoy the earth and all the products which result from it, 'with thanksgiving' (1 Tim 4:4,5), because they alone are fully in touch with the one who ultimately made it.

Property, material possessions, sex, beauty, creation and culture should be most appreciated and most wisely enjoyed by Christians. And, in excess of anyone else, Christians should love and care for those God loves (Matt 5:20). In our day, that will necessarily involve political and social action as well as evangelism and ordinary acts of service.

Furthermore, Paul makes it clear that the early Christians could not cut themselves off from unchristian society in order to keep themselves pure. If they wanted to do so they 'would have to leave this world' (1 Cor 5:10). They were thoroughly involved in the rough-and-tumble of ordinary living and did not retreat into a Christian enclave. The early Christians simply did not accept the option of indulging in the luxury of being an introverted holy huddle. They were members of mainstream culture, even if they always lived as strangers within it.

In the light of these points we must be careful not to misunderstand the New Testament. It calls for a firm rejection of secularism and of society in opposition to God. But our rejection must not be more scrupulous than God's. So much which God has given is good and can be affirmed.

To conclude, the fundamental ethos of the New Testament was undoubtedly less secular than our own. But the growth of secularism is a difference of degree rather than one of kind. The particular form of secularism we face is an advanced form of the virus. But in embryonic form it reveals itself in the New Testament and shows that the early Christians responded with a no-nonsense, no-compromise approach because they realized how fatal that virus could be.

PART THREE

Looking in the Mirror

6
The world
in the church

In Os Guinness's brilliant book *The Gravedigger File*, the
Deputy Director of the Central Security Council is writing
to the Director Designate of the Los Angeles Bureau about
the most effective way to undermine the church. He
comments, 'our best interests are served, not by working
against the church but by working with it'. It is all too easy
to see what he means.

The church often embraces contemporary culture and
accepts its basic ideas and values, only to find that in doing
so it has introduced subversive agents which threaten to
destroy it. Of course, if it realized what it was doing it
would be much more careful. But, then, if they had known
what they were doing the Trojans would have been more
cautious about welcoming that horse into their midst.

In what ways has the church speeded the progress of
secularization by its own worldliness?

Rationalism . . .

Being a Christian in a secular society demands the skills of
a tightrope walker. It is difficult to keep upright and reach
your destination without losing your balance. If you do
topple over you have a choice of two directions in which to
fall. One way or the other, Christians are always toppling
over into the abyss of secularism. On the one hand they do
so by over-emphasizing reason and falling into rationalism.
On the other hand they do so by over-emphasizing the
supernatural and falling into anti-intellectualism. The one
is the reverse mirror image of the other.

Reasons and evidences

In recent years, much effort has been invested in proving
the reasonableness of the Christian faith. Some have been
concerned to defend the historical reliability of the Bible
against sceptics. Some have sought to provide archaeological
justification for believing the Bible. Others have tried to
unravel some of the documentary difficulties and apparent
inconsistencies in the Bible itself, so that no unnecessary
stumbling-blocks are put in the way of the thinking person
to prevent him or her from believing.

Still others, showing great respect for contemporary
scholarship and the intellect, have been concerned to
demonstrate the reasonableness of Christianity on a broader
basis. Some have tried to square the teaching of the Bible
with recent scientific theories. Many have been concerned
to make its teaching philosophically acceptable. Yet others
have sought to reconcile the findings of psychologists and
sociologists with what the Bible teaches about man.

This approach to the defence of Christianity has much
to commend it. After all, God reveals himself to be a God
of truth. So one would not expect him to propagate a
message that either contained error or was based on error.
If error could be proved, then God should be doubted.
Conversely, the more evidence that passes muster as far as
the contemporary standards of intellectual life are

concerned, the better. Modern men, who show so much faith in reason, might be persuaded to believe. Furthermore, one would expect men and women, in pursuit of the mandate God their creator gave them, to discover truth as they investigate his world scientifically and in other ways.

The approach based on reason, however, too readily becomes an approach based on rationalism. Whereas reason is vital to the Christian faith, rationalism is suicidal. Rationalism is reason taken to the extreme. Reason is a useful tool, but in rationalism it has become the master. Rationalism opens the door wide to allow secularism to enter the church. How does that happen?

Two versions of rationalism

Rationalism comes in two guises: formal academic clothing and informal popular clothing.

The academic variety

In its academic garb, several dangers can be spotted.

Firstly, the evidence can become an end in itself. Rather than pointing to the need for faith in Jesus Christ, Christianity becomes merely another topic for debate, which enables scholars, typically, to avoid coming to any definite conclusions. 'Do you really believe in Adam and Eve?', 'Was Jonah really swallowed by a fish?', 'All religions lead to God, don't they?' and so on. For all the value of argument, people do not ultimately become Christians because they are persuaded intellectually. People become Christians because God opens their blinded eyes (2 Cor 4:4–6). Evangelism means engaging in spiritual warfare, not an intellectual exercise. If it ceases to be the former and degenerates into the latter, secularism has made a significant advance.

A second danger is that it allows man and his mind to be the ultimate umpire of what is and what is not to be believed. The whole assumption of rationalism is that man's mind is the ultimate authority. If Christianity passes through the filter of man's own philosophies and scientific theories, then it will be accepted. If it does not, then it will be discarded.

But man is ill-equipped to make such judgments. God's revelation is a surer basis to begin with than man's uncertain and partial discoveries.

Even Christians engage in this intellectual snobbery. Many enter at least a caveat about the teaching of the Bible about this or that until it has been passed fit by their scientific or philosophical framework. So, never mind the clear teaching of the Bible about the blessing of financial giving to the Lord's work (2 Cor 9:6–8), we are schooled into thinking that we should give only when we can safely afford it. We don't take risks in giving, especially when our income is low, and so we don't put God to the test (Mal 3:10). Rather we try to protect our scarce resources.

A third danger is that such an approach becomes so preoccupied with the natural world that it loses sight of the invisible world. It gets thoroughly engrossed in fossils and facts and is in danger of squeezing out faith. The natural order takes the centre of the stage while the supernatural order waits in the wings. Reason is better equipped to understand the former than the latter.

A fourth danger is that of hitching Christian theology to a passing intellectual star. When the star goes into eclipse, Christianity goes into eclipse with it. Science is always making advances, and the theories of today are replaced by the discoveries of tomorrow, some of which are extremely revolutionary. That is how it should be in science. But if Christianity is too closely linked with it then it becomes an anachronism as surely as the scientific theories of yesteryear. No one has expressed it better than Dean Inge (1860–1954) who once warned that, 'He who marries the spirit of this age will find himself a widower in the next.'

The popular variety
Leaving aside the rarefied atmosphere of the academics, we find that rationalism also has more comfortable clothes which it often wears to church.

Its most common popular style is the lack of any real

belief in the supernatural. If challenged, many church-going people would say that they believe in a living God who answers prayer and can work miracles. But they are as surprised – and just as sceptical – as anyone else when he does. Much of the time they do not even notice when God answers prayer. They simply take the answers for granted as the outworking of the natural order of things.

As for supernatural signs and wonders, interventions and miracles, they are just as cautious. Rather like their nineteenth-century predecessors who reacted to speaking in tongues and words of prophecy in the church of Edward Irving (1792–1834), they say, 'Yes, in theory God could do these things, but he isn't responsible for this lot.' For the most part, belief in a living, supernatural God is only a theoretical one. In practice, the world in which they live is as closed a system as that inhabited by the unbelieving scientist. And God has a hard time trying to break in.

The other popular style of rationalism has to do with doctrine. Rationalists believe that man's mind must be able to understand everything and tie up all the loose ends so that beliefs should be consistent. Doctrinal rationalists in the church have a very cerebral approach to Christianity and place a great stress on doctrinal correctness. Often they have a system of doctrine in which all the possible contradictions are ironed out, all the questions are answered and no loose ends (which if pulled could undo the whole system) are left untied. The only trouble is that they leave no room for the living God. They have him all tied up. He is domesticated and predictable. He does not go in for surprises – but he is very good at passing doctrinal examinations! Such sterile orthodoxy is a form of intellectualism in which, perversely, people have put their own minds in the position of supreme judge. That, as we have seen, opens the door to secularism.

Doctrine is important, and it really does matter what you believe, but in the Bible it is never divorced from living. Knowledge of God does not mean knowing about God, but a relationship with him which issues in obedience.

Science examinations usually involve a theoretical paper and a practical. Well, the Bible's understanding of knowledge always involves a practical. It is impossible to know about holiness without being holy. The trouble is the Western mind fails to grasp this. So we have the sorry spectacle of people who can tie us in knots over the theory of sanctification but live unlovely and unChristlike lives.

Christianity insists that both truth and experience are important. It has as much to do with enjoying a relationship with God and experiencing him in our lives as believing in correct doctrine. To divorce these two leads us into trouble.

Summary

All these approaches are in danger of placing too great an importance on the mind. But reason *is* a God-given faculty and should not be devalued. In the next section we shall see some of the perils of neglecting reason. Here we may note that the right use of reason is particularly important in our understanding of the Bible. Many evangelical Christians would simply want to take the Bible at face value and interpret it all literally. Mind you, they are curiously selective in doing so! So, they may well insist that their women wear hats (1 Cor 11:5) but they are unlikely to engage in much washing of feet (John 13:1-17). But if we use our reason aright, under the direction of the Holy Spirit, we shall be asking, What do these words mean? What did this passage originally mean to those to whom it was first addressed? What do we know about the context that will help us understand it? What form of language is being used; is it literal or poetic? What abiding principles are being taught?

The abandoning of reason has led to some very curious uses of the Bible indeed. But it must always be remembered that our ability to reason was warped by the fall, so reason alone is never to be wholly trusted. The Christian faith is founded, first and foremost, not on man's reason but on God's revelation.

... and its mirror image

Falling off the tightrope into rationalism is only one way to fall. The other is to fall into credulity – the reverse image of rationalism. Mainstream public culture may be based on rationalism, but minority cultures and private lives show a strong reaction against it. Rationalism can produce a very boring world, so it is not surprising that people should look for alternatives which are more exciting. When these people assess what to believe, feeling is made more important than fact, the subjective more important than the objective and experience more important than truth. Such an approach brings with it its own peculiar style in which spontaneity replaces structure, informality is stressed rather than formality and openness is valued above organization.

The charismatic corrective

Following the Second World War evangelicals fought for the reasonableness of Christianity by establishing themselves as credible scholars. But since the 1960s there has been a reaction against that cerebral approach to Christianity. The churches, like everyone else, have experienced a reaction against sterile intellectualism.

Few churches have been unaffected by the charismatic movement with its rediscovery of the supernatural gifts of the Spirit, its stress on actually experiencing God and its lively and spontaneous worship. Much of that has been a positive gain – a necessary correction to an earlier imbalance.

The demonstration of the supernatural has been vitally necessary in a closed world, which was devoted wholly to the natural. But the charismatic movement has not been a pure movement of the Spirit any more than any previous trend in the church has been. There have been elements in it which were mere reflections of the wider culture. And it too has been responsible for encouraging some to let in the spirit of the age.

Credulity and anti-intellectualism

On the debit side, some recent trends have been anti-intellectual. Serious study of the scriptures has been rejected in favour of a more immediate experience of God. Preaching has been devalued so that words of tongues and prophecy, often messages of little real consequence, can be given. Doctrine has been devalued and scholarship distrusted. The end result is that the mind has been replaced by the feelings as the ultimate judge of what is right and wrong. And that is certainly to jump out of the frying pan into the fire, for feelings are an even less reliable guide than the mind.

This anti-intellectualism has even been quite common among people with well-trained minds or in responsible graduate-type jobs. Many have shown a remarkable capacity to behave like schizophrenics. At work they use their minds, and wouldn't dream of doing otherwise. But then they disengage their minds and leave them at work to ensure that they do not interfere with their faith. Spiritual matters are apparently to be judged by wholly different criteria.

The difficulty with this is that in the end there are no criteria by which to judge whether something is right or wrong. Experience is a very unsatisfactory test. Experiences can be extremely convincing, yet counterfeit. It is not only Christians who speak in tongues or work miracles of healings. The devil delights to masquerade as an angel of light. Experiences can be simulated or manufactured. They need not be genuine. They need interpreting and can too easily be misinterpreted. They do not carry any weight with others who can reply dismissively, 'So what? That's you're experience, mine is different.'

The end product has often been a tendency to credulity. Enormous, and sometimes ludicrous, claims have been made about healings and prophecies which have not borne any close examination at all. People have been told that they were healed when manifestly they were not. 'Prophecies' have been given foretelling the birth of children – even sometimes of a certain sex – or of some impending calamity when neither child nor calamity have been forth-coming! On one occasion, which I have personally checked, a prophecy was given stating that a deceased believer would rise three days after his burial. But the body still lies in the grave awaiting the great resurrection day.

Yet even to question such words of prophecy or claims to healing has been to bracket oneself with the unbelievers. How different this is from the days of the Old Testament when prophets were tested and stoned if their prophecies did not come true (Deut 18:20–22), and where false dreams and visions were unmasked (Ezek 13:1–23). Similarly, the early Christians were told to test such supernatural inter-ventions to see if they really did come from God or not (1 Cor 14:29; 1 Thess 5:19–21; 1 John 4:1).

The attitude of some modern believers reminds one of Tertullian's unwise, if understandable, comment against the Gnostics, 'I believe because it is absurd.' In some people's eyes the more absurd, the greater the test of faith. This lack of discernment, and willingness to embrace anything out of the ordinary, leads not only to sensation-alism but to syncretism. In the absence of any solid Chris-tian theology, some sermons are more reminiscent of Hinduism than Christianity, and some testimonies of healing more reminiscent of Shintoism than the Gospels.

More wrong emphases

Also on the debit side, the over-emphasis on the Spirit and the supernatural has led to a devaluing of the material and the natural. So it has been considered of greater spiritual merit to be cured by the laying on of hands than by a doctor's prescription, or to be careless about one's employ-ment prospects and 'to live by faith' than to plan respon-sibly for the future, or to be guided by a dream than by circumstances.

At a deeper level, creation itself has been devalued. The spirit is all that matters. But curiously that has led people in two opposite directions. On the one hand they have thought that even noticing creation was sinful, so they have eschewed good clothes, shunned culture, refrained from spending time and money on leisure pursuits and even avoided sex. On the other hand some have said that since the material does not matter they can indulge themselves in it and enjoy it freely, even, in some cases, to the extent of riding roughshod over God's moral laws. The spirit is all that counts, not the body.

Private enterprise?

Perhaps the point where secularism has been embraced the most is in the reinforcement of religion as a purely private affair. God is spoken of as a God of great power, but the power seems almost wholly directed to the individual. Testimonies abound as to the way God has healed backache or emotional scars, as to how he provided parking spaces at convenient points, kept the weather fine for a church event, and provided money or even one's favourite fruit-juice on journeys. But little is said about God's concern for the starving, or about social injustice, racial hatred or violence between nations. To the uninvolved observer God seems more limited there. Politicians are ignored and the public world is met with a deafening silence. Such an approach confirms and augments one of secularization's most powerful and dynamic aspects – that religion is a leisure-time choice which has nothing serious to say to the real world. The gulf between the public and private worlds is widened even further. The church is privately engaging but socially irrelevant. And secularization can go from strength to strength.

Rationalization

Secularization not only involves rationalism but rationalization. Rationalism has to do with *the way we think* whereas rationalization has to do with *the methods we adopt*. The one is a natural implication of the other.

The pressure of technology forces us in the direction of

rationalization. Tasks have to be systematized, standardized, repeatable, concentrated and centralized. There is little room for the personal or the individual; they are regarded as eccentric and inconvenient. Bucking the system is frowned upon. Take, for example, getting photographs developed. It is easy to get colour prints developed because the machines are all set up to go; you can have them back, in a limited choice of standard forms and sizes, in no time. But if you want to get a black and white film developed, you throw the system. It will take you far longer and cost you far more than it would have done in the days before mechanization.

Rationalization in the church

The same trend towards rationalization is evident in the church. In themselves, the expressions of this trend may all seem eminently sensible. The trouble is that behind them lies a way of thinking which tends towards secularism, yet we do not even realize it. What are we thinking of?

Our approach to evangelism

Take evangelism. Since the days of Charles Finney (1792–1875) we have become more and more rationalized in our approach to it. Until Finney, men believed that revival was a sovereign work of God's Holy Spirit and, although we should seek it, there was nothing we could do to bring it about. Finney taught that revival could be experienced if only men would fulfil the right conditions. He came up, more or less, with a formula. A little of this and a lot of that combined with something else and God would not be able to hold back. Revival would break out.

Formula thinking now permeates the whole of evangelism. If God doesn't save people, it is because we got the equation wrong and we didn't pray enough, have enough faith or do enough visiting. The onus is on us, rather than on God. Just like any good salesman, when we do evangelism we have a structured conversation which enables us to deal with all the objections, handle all the awkward customers and anticipate all the information they need to know.

When God does save someone, we have a clear system to tell them what to do. So there are four spiritual laws they need to hear or a packaged system of steps they need to take. We can guarantee success if they go through the system properly. And, once they are saved, we have the ten steps to maturity ready to hand to enable them to grow up quickly. Holiness and devotion are codified and the 'How-to . . .' manuals will quickly produce the required results if followed carefully enough.

I do not intend to knock them, since I know that many of these systems have been of great help to many Christians and enabled many to have confidence as evangelists that they would otherwise lack. But we also know that our formulas have often not worked, because people cannot be packaged that simply and God can be packaged even less. People are gloriously different individuals and God, as a creator of infinite variety, meets each one of them differently, in his grace.

Our approach to church structures and planning
Our belief in rationalization shows itself in numerous other ways. On a national scale we see it with the increasing trend towards centralization in our denominations and even in the house churches. The Paul Report, written in the 1960s, grappled with the problems of plant and shortage of manpower in the Church of England by applying normal management techniques to the problems. It was a classic expression of rationalization.

But every church has indulged in its own similar exercise since then. The closure of churches or the uniting of small ones is just what you would expect of a church run on lines of business management. Agreements are reached as to which denomination should open a church in a new town or on a new housing estate, as in a standard business cartel.

Similarly, church growth thinking approaches the mission of the church by using the recent discoveries of the human sciences to enable the church to exploit to the full its scarce resources and to maximize its results.

Once again, we are not intending to imply that all these approaches are beyond redemption. Some of them are a necessary and legitimate response to the age in which we live. But we easily cross the fine line between using them as a tool of God and making them our masters. We need to recognize their secularizing potential in order that we stay the right side of the line.

On a more local level, too, we often act in this rationalizing, secular fashion without realizing it. Our planning is often no more than human strategy. 'Strategy committees' are concerned exclusively with money and buildings. Faith and prayer don't come into it. Yet without either money or buildings in their strategy the early church made an enormous impact on their world.

Having visions and dreaming dreams is a mark of the age of the Spirit (Acts 2:17). But we feel safer with committees and consultations. We often lack the faith to deal in the dimension of the invisible, preferring only to deal in the visible resources we know we have. Rather than engaging in spiritual warfare we feel much more confident if we leave things to human engineering. This is, of course, a caricature, but it is sufficiently close to the real thing to be uncomfortable and to expose how deep secularism is in our thinking.

Our approach to people
Our attitude to people sometimes betrays the secularism in our hearts as well.

If the rich young ruler had come to us, instead of to Jesus, we would have almost certainly been so impressed by his status, learning and wealth that we would have instantly co-opted him to the diaconate or the PCC. But Jesus sent him away.

James 2 may instruct us to show impartiality to all men whether rich or poor, and we would never engage in the sort of crude prejudice which he condemns. But in a thousand subtle ways we still make the socially acceptable more welcome in the church than the poor.

We cannot say with Paul, 'So from now on we regard no-one from a worldly point of view' (2 Cor 5:16). Human rationality abounds at the expense of spiritual wisdom.

Narcissism

Self-worship

In the Greek myth, Narcissus angered the goddess Artemis by refusing to fall head over heels in love with Echo. Artemis was so annoyed that she punished him by causing him to fall in love with his own reflection in a fountain. Narcissus did not find it a wholesome experience and eventually, in despair, he took his own life. His name has been linked with self-worship ever since.

We have seen how Paul denounced self-worship in 2 Timothy 3:1-5, describing it as the religion of the last days. No more accurate picture could be given of much of the religion of our own day than that. Much contemporary worship is pure narcissism and many recent trends are nakedly narcissistic. We do not see them as such since they are thinly disguised by a veneer of Christianity, but peel that off and not far underneath is pure 'selfism'.

Self-centredness in contemporary society

There has been a profound change in society since the second world war. Broadly speaking, until that time people were happy to fulfil social roles and were oriented towards others in their thinking and behaviour. Even if they were not happy with the situation they accepted it. But since the 1960s we have become much more self-directed. We are motivated by self-fulfilment rather than social obligation. 'I have a duty to myself' and 'I must be true to my own self' are the catch-phrases of the age.

According to Alvin Toffler in *The Third Wave*, this is a logical outcome of our industrial way of life. In the technological sphere we atomize everything. In society we have done the same. The basic unit is no longer the tribe, clan or even the family, but the individual – autonomous and free, yet empty.

In relation to responsibilities

A superficial illustration of this process can be seen in family life. Rather than accepting the obligations of family relationships – say, as a son or daughter with responsibility for ageing parents, as a husband and wife in lifelong commitment, or as a father and mother towards our children – we contrive to break free from them.

Some ways of shelving the responsibilities are less messy than others. Old people's homes are an acceptable convenience, divorce is common but painful, while one-parent families are a major source of strain all round and most of all to the one parent left with the children. But thrusting the individual into prominence like this has even deeper implications for his psychology and his religion.

In the solutions to loneliness

God never intended man to live in such isolation from his fellow men. As John Milton pointed out, loneliness was the first thing in the world God pronounced 'not good'. The individualism creates a void which men desperately try to fill.

Sometimes, on the rebound, they do so by entering a well-structured, authoritarian community where they experience the family that contemporary society denied them. Most often, however, they try to fill the void without giving up the root cause, the individualism itself. So instead of turning outwards they turn inwards and through meditation techniques, psychological therapies, encounter groups, human potential movements and assertiveness training they try to release their real selves.

Feeling good matters; so allied to all the mental strategies for self-fulfilment come yoga, aerobics, dieting, vegetarianism and various beauty therapies. Even courses aimed

at enhancing relationships within marriage often pander to
the need for the individual to be more fulfilled.

Self-centredness in the church

The church has imbibed the spirit of this age. The explosive
growth of counselling courses and techniques bears witness
to it. In Os Guinness's words, 'Firm belief is a matter of
aerobics rather than apologetics, of human fitness rather
than divine faithfulness. Shapeliness is next to godliness.'
Guidance is usually settled on the principle of, 'I felt peace
about it', without ever apparently realizing that some things
God may be calling us to may be uncomfortable and costly.

In popular Christian literature

A review of popular Christian books easily demonstrates
how self-centred we have become. One survey in the United
States included endless titles such as *God's Key to Health and
Happiness, The Art of Understanding Yourself, Transformed
Temperaments, Psychology of Jesus and Mental Health, You
Can Change Your Personality, Do I Have to Be Me?, I Want
Happiness Now, How to Get Through Your Struggles, You
and Your Husband's Mid-life Crisis, Feeling Good About
Feeling Bad, Relax and Live Longer, You Can Become the
Person You Want to Be, Happiness: You Can Find the Secret,
How to Become Your Own Best Self.* The survey, conducted
by James Hunter Davidson, investigated eight major evangelical publishers in the USA and concluded that only
12.2% of their books approached people's problems from
the viewpoint of traditional Christian teaching. The rest
offered a Christianized variation of recent psychology, in
one form or another.

Davidson admits that the narcissism found among evangelicals is different from that in the broader American
culture which, in its crudest form, says, 'If it feels good,
do it.' Evangelicals talk of releasing the potential of the
human being under the Lordship of Christ. Similarly, the
quest for pleasure is disguised in Christian terms, such as,
'Jesus meant the Christian life to be exciting.' But the

preoccupation with self, with ironing out all inner suffering, with ease, with a trouble-free and fulfilled life is still plain.

In prosperity teaching
Others advocate a gospel of prosperity where the blessings of 3 John 2, 'I pray that you may enjoy good health and that all may go well with you, even as your soul is getting along well,' are sought literally. But the quality of life enjoyed by those advocates seems to differ little, if at all, from their secular counterparts. Often they merely seem to reflect the idols of the society in which they live.

Such narcissism stands in sharp contrast to the New Testament's preoccupation with the will of God, expressed in service to others and the willing acceptance of suffering and the cross. It is a reflection of the secularism of our age.

Just as rationalism produces its own reverse image, so does narcissism. Some Christians rebound from the self-indulgent spirit of the churches, into a new authoritarianism where they are willing to subject themselves to anything as proof of their desire for holiness.

Summary

These are only the main ways in which secularism puts a foot in the door of the church. Each characteristic trend which we have reviewed contains aspects which are positively right and helpful to the church. The trouble comes when they are adopted uncritically.

Minds matter. But the mind is not everything. Subjective experience is valid – but not alone. Rationalization can make spiritual sense. But it may equally open the door to a church dominated by human wisdom. God longs to fill the vacuum in the deepest recesses of our damaged personalities. But we can too easily end up worshipping ourselves instead of him. We need to be aware of the secularizing potential each of these features possesses before we let the chain off and throw the door open too widely in welcome.

7
The church
in the world

Future shock

It is hard to remember what the world was like as little as
twenty-five years ago. The last two decades have been
decades of unprecedented change. A person who died at
the end of the 1950s would find today's world almost
unrecognizable.

The bewildering pace and variety of change
Change occurs relentlessly in every area of our lives. The
degree of change is so much that many are punch-drunk as
a result. Alvin Toffler has described our condition as one
of 'future shock' because, he says, we are suffering from
the premature arrival of the future.

Technological changes
Many of the changes have taken place because of
technology.

The television is in almost every home, and now dominates patterns of leisure. Throughout the 1950s it was a

luxury item, not an essential part of the furniture.

Other technological leisure equipment has mushroomed. The record-player gave away to the hi-fi and then to the compact disc. The tape recorder gave way to the cassette and then the Walkman. The wireless gave way to the transistor radio and then to the watch radio. The lantern slide gave way to the colour slide, then to the home movie and now to the video.

Such changes have profound social effects in the areas of family life and patterns of leisure. But they are trivial in comparison with other ways in which our consciousness has been expanded.

In 1956 Sir Richard Woolley, then Astronomer Royal, said, 'Space travel is utter bilge.' But in 1969 Neil Armstrong stepped out of his lunar module and walked on the moon. In fact space travel is so much taken for granted that it takes a tragedy of the order of the 1986 *Challenger* disaster, when the space shuttle blew up, killing all seven of its crew, even to notice that it is going on.

Great advances have also taken place in micro-technology, bringing resources and abilities which previous generations never knew existed, and would certainly have failed to comprehend, within the reach of everyone. So, for example, a whole generation of children are at home with computers in a way which makes their parents feel distinctly uneasy.

Nuclear experimentation has now become an uneasy but ever-present fact of life. As natural resources of energy, such as coal, gas and oil, have threatened to run out, so governments have been forced to explore nuclear energy. But in addition to the widespread revulsion at its evil and destructive potential in warfare, there has been an ongoing sense of disquiet about its safety in everyday life.

Social changes

Immense social changes have taken place.

Education underwent a massive expansion in the late 1960s so that undreamt of opportunities were made available to those previously denied access to higher education. Equal opportunities became bywords of the age. Almost simultaneously, changes took place in the style of education: rote learning was replaced by an emphasis on understanding; being told was replaced by the need to discover for oneself, and finding answers was replaced by asking questions.

Then there was the rise of immigration. Although usually grossly overestimated as far as numbers were concerned (by 1976 only just over 3% of the British population were black, and 40% of these were born in Britain), it challenged the cosy and coherent culture of white Britain and brought fear and prejudice to the surface. New patterns of culture inevitably had to be forged.

More recently there is the fact of unemployment. Since the war, changes have taken place leading to the decline of traditional heavy industries such as ship-building, wool and cotton manufacturing and steel making. But the revolution which is now upon us, thanks to micro-technology, is of an altogether different order. It has created a permanent unemployment force of over three millions – it is doubtful if we can ever return to full employment again, no matter how many consumer booms we might experience.

None of these changes could have taken place without profound moral consequences, and it is true that the last quarter of a century has seen a massive moral and spiritual upheaval.

Revised morals
The 1960s were a colourful adolescent age which questioned everything and knocked all existing institutions and morals.

The change in the leadership of the BBC was symptomatic of wider changes in society. Lord Reith had been a pillar of the establishment who sought to use the BBC to elevate the moral tone of the nation and educate its people in the ways of their fathers. His successor, Sir Hugh Carlton Greene, was an agnostic who explicitly stated that he, together with others, was going to knock the establishment and question the status quo and, in his words, 'my, oh, my, we are going to have fun doing so'. So unheard of words and unthought of programmes saw the light of day and became acceptable. Sex, rather than being an unmentionable subject, became an obligatory feature of every TV evening. Greene found a ready audience, for there was a general relaxation of sexual and moral codes at the time.

This growing permissiveness was abetted by advances in medical technology. The pill became a common means of contraception, and with it sexual intercourse was no longer restrained by the fear of an unwanted pregnancy. Moral principles were therefore under pressure to give way to expediency. Why restrain yourself if you did not have to?

Rigorous moral standards were further eased by a Parliament which reformed existing laws so that abortion and homosexual activity between consenting adults were no longer offences. Shortly afterwards, embryo technology was to raise a whole new set of moral dilemmas. In the 1960s and 1970s, the quest for sexual satisfaction was paralleled to a worrying degree by those who sought ecstasy through drugs.

The squeezing out of religion
Meanwhile Parliament gave less and less credence to religion. Thus, although an act of Christian worship and the teaching of religion in schools is obligatory under the 1944 Education Act, it is widely and blatantly disregarded without comment. The *Times Educational Supplement* recently reported that less than 2.4% of schools held a full daily assembly as the law requires. Conversely, should a bishop in the House of Lords wish to make a moral point touching on politics, he is quickly branded as a covert party political spokesman and told to keep his nose out.

The humanist lobby

How have all these changes come about? Largely because of a small but powerful group who have espoused humanism as the philosophy which fits the new age. Their persuasive lobbying means that we now define our values and morals by a new frame of reference. They are no longer defined by reference to God, the Bible, tradition or the church, but by ourselves, pure and simple.

Humanistic beliefs

Humanism comes in many shapes and forms, but it is possible to identify some major common themes which all humanists share.

They believe in man. Man is progressing all the time and has the capabilities within himself to solve his own problems and improve his lot. Evolution, one of the cardinal doctrines of humanism, will ensure that the progress continues. Man is not a spiritual being who needs to refer to an outside source. In fact, according to a spokesman like the famous British philosopher and social activist, Bertrand Russell (1872–1970), it is their false dependence on God which has made the churches the chief enemy of moral progress in the world.

Humanists believe that this world is all that there is. There is no evidence, they say, for life after death. Man is no more than a biological organism who operates in a particular social and cultural context. So he need have no concern for a future life or judgment. Nor dare he believe that the evils of this world will be righted in the next. They must be put right now. The injustices of poverty, ignorance and disease must be overcome now, or not at all. Since man will not survive death, his concern must be wholly with this life.

The implications of humanism

All this has implications for the way we make our moral decisions. Morality must be worked out without reference to God. As an autonomous being, man must come to his own conclusions. No outside standard or threat of judgment is relevant. Ethical standards do not need to be justified by theology. The humanists' first commitment is to free enquiry, without the restraint of taboo areas and fixed ideas imposed by the church.

Thus in 'A Secular Humanist Declaration', published in the magazine *Free Inquiry* a few years ago, it was stated that, 'Secular humanism places trust in human intelligence rather than in divine guidance . . .' Humanists do not claim to have got 'the answers' by this means. Rather, they doubt whether there is any such thing as 'the answer'. This explains the declaration's statement: 'We do not believe that any one church should impose its views on moral virtue and sin, sexual conduct, marriage, divorce, birth control, or abortion, or legislate them for the rest of society.' For a humanist, ethical and moral decisions must always be provisional, relative and situational. They are determined by the consequences not by any principles. There can be no absolute standards. Ideas will change according to time, culture and circumstance.

Our recent history would suggest that while the churches apparently do not have the right to legislate morals, the humanists do!

The Christian response

Where do we as Christians stand in all this? There are a number of positions which we might adopt, and which the churches have adopted over the years. As we review those positions, we shall ask: What is the most appropriate position now?

The imposition of moral and spiritual values?

In the first place, the church might seek to dominate culture and impose its moral and spiritual values on the nation. We can see this in the Roman Catholic Church in Ireland or in the approach of the Moral Majority in America. Israel, in the Old Testament, serves as the model for this view. Though they could be distinguished, the sacred infused what we would now call the secular with its values. So although we may divide the law into its religious, moral or social aspects, the ancient Israelites did not. To them, the whole of the law, whether giving regulations for worship, family life or health, demonstrated the will of their creator.

This view takes seriously the claim of God on all life and all his creatures, whether they acknowledge him or not. For a long time it was the position in Britain as church and culture were almost indistinguishable.

For centuries the established church played a major role in legislating for moral behaviour and was actively consulted and listened to when any moral dilemma was faced. But there were also numerous ways in which it influenced culture more widely and ensured that only people who held its views could exercise any real influence in the nation. So, for example, until the mid-nineteenth century only Anglicans could gain access to Oxford and Cambridge, the universities which provided the nation with most of its aristocracy, politicians, diplomats and other leading figures. Before the rise of popular newspapers the church had the virtual monopoly of the means of communication. And the church had a large hand in the exercise of social control through the courts.

Although this degree of control still persists in some countries where Roman Catholicism is the dominant religion, it is clear that it is no longer viable in Britain. If we think it is, we are living with our heads in the sand. The social fabric of our nation has changed and no church here is in the position it was. To a great extent the social position of the established church is a relic of the past and does not fit with the social realities of the present. The legal position regarding the teaching of RE compared with the actual position to be found in schools, to which we have referred, epitomizes the situation. But even if this option were possible, history might make us question whether it was the right way forward.

The New Testament church was never in the position of imposing itself on its surrounding culture. Yet it had a massive spiritual, moral and social impact.

So, for example, it was simply not in a position to challenge slavery as a social institution, still less to legislate against it. But it quietly undermined it from within because of the new relationships masters and slaves discovered in Christ. And this was eventually reflected in legislation.

The same could be said of the observance of Sunday as a day of worship, or of principles of family life or of virtually any other area you care to choose.

It was not until the Roman emperor Constantine was converted that the church was placed in a privileged position in society and its ideals were imposed on others through legislation. Many would question whether this was a good thing since it also had the effect of adulterating Christianity by encouraging all sorts of people to jump on its bandwagon for ulterior reasons, and this eventually cut the spiritual nerve at the heart of the faith.

A more recent example might come from America. The United States has a rich Puritan heritage. At the turn of the century, when many moral decisions were up for grabs, attempts were made to ensure that it remained loyal to its inheritance. Through crusades, the courts and legislation, a vigorous group of Reformed theologians tried to impose their spiritual values on others. But they failed. One recent study of the period suggests that the chief cause of their failure was that they adopted the wrong strategy. Gary Scott Smith has argued that it was precisely because they were spiritual imperialists, trying to dominate the culture and admit no alternatives, that they were rejected. Had they been prepared to adopt an approach more in keeping with the pluralistic context of their day, they might have been more influential. Their religious monopoly, like ours, was over.

Withdrawal from the world?
A second position might be the opposite extreme – a withdrawal from engaging in the world altogether. Many Christians, such as the Christian Brethren among whom I grew

up and to whom I owe much, have adopted this position over the years.

At the shallowest end, some felt that 'this world is not my home, I'm just a passing through', and so treated the world with complete indifference. Their eyes were firmly fixed on heaven and what went on here on earth was irrelevant.

At the deep end, some thought that the dispensation in which they were living meant that the world would get worse and worse and that there was nothing they either could or should do to rescue it. The worse the world got, the more they were confirmed in their view that they were right to be uninvolved because, on the basis of passages like 2 Timothy 4:1–5 or 2 Peter 2 and 3, the faster the world degenerated the faster the Lord would return.

A cluster of other arguments range around this position. The New Testament, it is said, never gives Christians any encouragement to get involved in politics. The public world is a dirty world and would cause the Christian to get contaminated. Christians, however, must keep themselves 'from being polluted by the world' (Jas 1:27). The world is in the grip of the evil one and is controlled by spiritual authorities which are opposed to God. The only way for us to relate to it, therefore, is by not relating to it – to wash our hands of it.

But this is to be too negative about the world. Although it rightly brings one side of biblical truth to our attention, it ignores the other side which needs to be held in tension.

God has not abdicated his responsibility as creator. He still sends his rain on the just and the unjust. As the salt of the earth, we are there to preserve the world from corruption and delay its decay as long as possible, even if its final destination is already fixed (Matt 5:13–16).

A total biblical perspective would help us to see that God's mercy is wider than just saving the elect. The Old Testament prophets, with their emphasis on the need for all nations – not just Israel – to be righteous, would become our examplees. And we would take Paul's words seriously when he said, 'as we have opportunity, let us do good to all people . . .' (Gal 6:10). We would also remember Paul's sensible comment, already mentioned, that if we want to separate ourselves consistently from all unbelievers then we might as well get in our space-ships and leave the earth (1 Cor 5:10). Even if it were right, it could not be done.

Withdrawal from the world is both to neglect spiritual duties which God has given us and, from a practical viewpoint, to pursue a foolish road. Unlike the early Christians, we live in a democracy. It would have made no sense to tell *them* to get involved in politics. But as citizens we have a duty and opportunity to do so, and we may affect our nation for good if we do. Remember the old saying, 'All that is needed to let evil flourish is for good men to do nothing.'

Again, to withdraw is to pursue a foolish road because the end product is that Christians live together in an introverted sect and so lose the ability to communicate with their fellow citizens, even about the Lord.

There are plenty of examples of small groups who have decided to withdraw and let the world pass them by. Eventually, these sects have either become extinct or, if they haven't, they have become historical oddities who could only talk among themselves but not to outsiders. A few, by their radical differences from mainline society, have stood as a powerful sign of another world. But they are the rare exceptions. The New Testament does not encourage us to move in the direction of withdrawal.

Identifying with culture?
The third position we might adopt is to seek agreement between our Christianity and contemporary culture and is commonly found among churches of a more liberal orientation. This has both a positive and a negative aspect to it.

Positively, we can see the way in which the Christian faith, by co-operating with contemporary movements, can improve the lot of mankind. Thus, the advancement of education, the progress of medical science and the liberation of women, may or may not have stemmed initially from specifically Christian movements. But by seeking points of identity between them and the Christian gospel and advocating them from a Christian viewpoint their cause may be advanced. Society may be improved as a result.

In a more superficial way, too, there may be value in seeking agreement between Christianity and culture. It saves us from trying to preserve the wrong things, such as a certain language, music, dress or other customs, which have more to do with the culture of a past generation than with the Christian gospel. Every generation needs to cut back the cultural undergrowth to allow the beauty of the gospel to be seen afresh. Every generation needs to learn to communicate the one gospel in a contemporary way.

Sadly, however, this position may be more negative than positive, and often has been. In practice it often means that Christian truth is eroded by contemporary society and churches end up merely parroting the latest fashion. When this happens, churches have lost their God-given distinctiveness. They are like sand-dunes, shaped by all the forces around them but having no active effect of their own on the surroundings. Rather than Christianizing the nation, which this approach seeks to do, it ends up secularizing the church.

Recent examples show how subtle this temptation can be. For instance, our society has defined freedom and tolerance as key virtues. The church does not wish to dissent from that emphasis. Why should it, when much of the original impetus to establish those principles as virtues derived from the church? But the danger is that the church then feels itself under an obligation to baptize every move towards tolerance and to bend over backwards to show itself enlightened. So recent church reports have spoken of adultery as a sacramental act of love and of homosexuality as a legitimate expression of sexuality, church authorities have been loath to condemn obscenity on the stage or screen, and the exclusiveness of Christianity and the preaching of hell have been muted because such doctrines are ill-at-ease in a tolerant age.

Another way in which the danger can be seen is that church authorities have often readily picked up a passing political fad and made it central to the Christian message in a way which results in mammon replacing God and the temporal being in sharper focus than the eternal. This approach needs to be watched with care.

Healthy resistance?

The fourth position is that of healthy resistance. In this position Christians are encouraged to be involved in the world but not sucked into it. This position is the one I believe to be most in line with scripture and the most realistic about our situation. It can be seen most clearly expressed in groups like the Mennonites, the Sojourners Community, or Care Trust.

It holds in tension the biblical view of the world: as God's creation on the one hand, and yet governed by the prince of the power of the air on the other. It takes a full biblical perspective and gives place to the Old Testament prophets as well as teaching about the need to keep oneself unstained by the world. It recognizes that God's concern is with righteousness and not just with individual salvation. It captures the New Testament vision that to live as a Christian would mean that there would be an overspill of God's love to those well outside the Christian circle.

This position is realistic. It admits that Christians have no monopoly on morals, nor can they enforce their views on others.

We live in a pluralistic society and must accept that others have a right to put their viewpoint. But that makes it imperative that we voice our opinions as citizens too. The nation would be poorer if we did not. Pluralism actually invites us to speak rather than be silent.

If we fail to speak, we will only be confirming people's view of the world as secular. But if we continuously and courteously say that we interpret the world differently, then, whether they accept our interpretation or not, we are standing as a witness to the supernatural and preventing secularism from a complete take-over. We shall be a bit like the old cathedral spires that point heavenwards.

If the strategy of healthy resistance is realistic, we must be realistic too, not least in our thinking as to what can be achieved and how we are to go about it.

Politics, being the art of the possible, involves compromise. We must be prepared to meet people part-way. We must also recognize that on many issues there is not 'a Christian position', but there are several Christian positions. A single, united Christian political party is therefore not an option, but there may well be several different ways of achieving the Christian goal we seek. We can speak about moral rights and wrongs, spiritual principles and eternal values, so what we ought to do is to inject Christian principles into all discussions.

William Temple, a former Archbishop of Canterbury, set out this position clearly in his wartime book *Christianity and the Social Order* (1942). He argued that it was not the church's role to dictate actual policies, but it was the church's role to advocate the ends which the social order should achieve and to criticize existing means if they were not achieving those ends. In a famous example he wrote:

> If a bridge is to be built, the church must remind the engineer that it is his obligation to provide a really safe bridge; but it is not entitled to tell him whether, in fact, his design meets this requirement . . . In just the same way the church may tell the politician what ends the social order should promote; but it must leave to the politician the devising of the precise means to those ends.

Let us take the issue of abortion as an example. It would be foolish to think that we could ever impose a pre–1929 position, when abortion was illegal, on the country again – even if Christians were united in wishing to do so. In fact, although Christians would share a widespread concern over the way the current law operates, not all would be agreed that abortion is always indisputably wrong. Yet as Christians we must be concerned about the sanctity of life and about the way man, through the practice of abortion, is usurping the role of life-giver and life-taker which belongs to God alone.

Shouting texts at our politicians, even if we could find those which related directly to abortion, will get us nowhere. Healthy resistance means that we should engage in intelligent and well-informed debate, listen sympathetically to others – especially women who adamantly insist on their right to abortion – argue the case on spiritual, medical, social and psychological grounds and be prepared to accept a compromise in the end.

The sort of compromise we might hope for would be that abortions would not be permitted after twenty weeks instead of twenty-eight weeks as at present, or that the present law remains but that its application be subject to much stricter interpretation. This would not only save thousands of otherwise wasted lives but give greater emphasis to the principle that life is God-given and sacred.

It also means we must put our money where our mouth is and do something to relieve the distress of the many women who are desperate for abortions because they can't cope with their present situation and can't bear the thought of adding the burden of another offspring to their load. The implications of this for Christians are immense; better marriage preparation, more faithful teaching regarding sexual and family life, more practical support for one-parent families and so on.

In other words, this position needs to be adopted with care. We need to engage in *healthy* resistance, not negative, pernickety and continuous opposition. We need to pick our battle areas with care and for their spiritual and strategic importance. Many Christians do not do that; instead, just like Catherine wheels, they fire off in all directions at once at every minute issue and, just like the Catherine wheel, they quickly become spent.

We must also adopt the healthy resistance approach with a great deal of humility. In the past Christians have often opposed certain things only to end up advocating them.

Sometimes, as in the case of Galileo, there has been an about turn because they have received a genuine new understanding. But sometimes they have merely given in.

Take an illustration to which the theologian Robin Gill has drawn attention: contraception. In 1908 the Anglican bishops condemned the use of contraception as 'demoralizing to character and hostile to national welfare'. In 1920 they said that it threatened the race and should be opposed on theological grounds. However, in 1930 they opened the door a fraction to the use of contraceptives. And by 1958 they said that 'planning was a positive choice before God'. Whatever the rights and wrongs of the various positions adopted, it reminds us that we need to speak with care, even when we confine ourselves to principles.

The world will not like it when we do speak for God. But what is new about that? The world will not like it because it cuts at the root of secularism. If secularism can confine religion to a private, leisure-time pursuit it is happy. But once religion breaks out of its confines and starts speaking about the real world secularism is under threat. So, to use Os Guinness's picture, the humanist security guards will frisk us to ensure that we don't get into the real world with our spiritual weapons. But, regardless of the risks, we need to be holy terrorists as well as holy diplomats.

The much maligned Bishop of Durham, David Jenkins, when criticized for making forays into the political arena, has said in his own defence that the crucial thing is not that people agree with him but that he has got the debate going. Perhaps he is right. It is a tragedy that in a so-called open society we Christians absent ourselves from the real world.

We frequently see the absurd spectacle of party politicians saying that the church should keep its nose out of politics. Such a claim is ludicrous. We might as well say that God should keep his nose out of the world! But we are equally absurd when we do not use the opportunities God *has* given, because we are then letting secularism have its own way. If we stop speaking for God, the window to the world beyond will get smaller and smaller until people will no longer see that there is a window there at all.

PART FOUR

Looking for Help

8
Living in exile:
Daniel

Imagine being just about twenty-two years old when an enemy power succeeds in defeating your country in war. The foreign army seizes everything worth taking and lays waste the rest. Fine buildings are destroyed. The nation's long heritage and culture lie in ruins. The government is put in prison and many other prisoners of war are taken. And the young men with the most potential, you included, are taken off to the other side of the world so that they can be indoctrinated with the alien culture of their oppressors. Hard to imagine? Maybe. But that is just what happened to Daniel and his friends Shadrach, Meshach and Abednego.

For Daniel and others, the events surrounding the fall of Jerusalem in 587 BC must have been a personal tragedy. What was their future to be? All that talent, all that skill, all that potential and all those personalities – were they just to be thrown on the scrap heap?

But the personal crisis which resulted from the exile was nothing in comparison with the spiritual crisis which resulted. The outward conditions in which they lived in captivity, at least to begin with, were fairly liberal. But inwardly they were prisoners of broken hearts and spiritual uncertainties. Psalm 137 movingly expresses their pain:

> By the rivers of Babylon we sat and wept
>   when we remembered Zion.
> There on the poplars
>   we hung our harps,
> for there our captors asked us for songs,
>   our tormentors demanded songs of joy;
>   they said, 'Sing us one of the songs of Zion!'
> How can we sing the songs of the Lord
>   while in a foreign land?

Where was God? Had he deserted them? Was he perhaps never more than a myth? Had he not promised to secure the throne of David for ever? Why had he not done so? Was he incapable of doing so and were his words so many empty promises? Or perhaps he was never there?

The exiles were unlikely to have responded to such questions with pure secularism. But their living in exile has a number of parallels to our living in an alien secular culture, not least in that the exiles were deported to a pluralistic culture. The Babylonians believed in gods all right, they believed in hundreds of them! Babylon alone had fifty-three temples, fifty-five shrines dedicated to Marduk, their chief god, 900 shrines dedicated to an assortment of other earthly or heavenly divinities, 180 altars to Ishtar and another 192 altars to further deities. And that was only the public face of religion. Each man would have had his own personal deity. It was religion of the liquorice all-sorts variety.

What confusion that must have produced and what temptation it brought in its train! Babylon must have seemed so grand and sophisticated when compared with Jerusalem. The empire was so great and powerful when contrasted with the backwater of Judah. They must have been greatly tempted to forget the Jewish faith and convert to Babylonian religion. In that situation it was difficult to see Yahweh, the God of the Jews, both literally and metaphorically. There was no idol you could point out named

Yahweh, whereas the Babylonians must have had their idols and temples on every street corner. But more significantly, they could not see their God at work in their own history. He was a hidden God. The gods of the Babylonians, however, seemed to have the upper hand and to have been powerful enough to control events, making their nation successful, and defeating Judah.

Then they faced the pressure to conform. Sometimes it was an explicit, forceful pressure. Conformity to state religion could be enforced by troops, prison, torture and even death. Powerful incentives to give up their distinctiveness! But even when it was not explicit there was the social pressure to conform. Daily life in Babylon revolved around the gods. Even if they did not want to submit, there was still the question of how they could remain faithful to the true God in such an alien environment. The old traditions and practices of religion were no longer relevant. The temple was not to hand, the calendar was not under their control, the sacrifices were no longer permissible and the priests could no longer function in the same way. What did faithfulness mean?

It was into this murky pool that Daniel and his friends were thrown and had to work out answers to many of the questions which forcefully confront us today. The opening chapters of Daniel give us clues as to how we ought to live while exiled in a secular society, each chapter teaching a new lesson.

Learning to draw the line (chapter 1)

Daniel and his friends came from the intellectual and social cream of Jewish society (3,4) and so were immediately marked out to be trained for public office. That is a nice way of putting it, for, in reality, they were to go through a process of thought reform which should have resulted in them being good conformist Babylonians inhabiting Jewish skins. They were to be carefully educated (4). Believing that every man has his price, the Babylonians gave these young men privileges (5) and hoped that these would still their defecting consciences. Interestingly enough, another feature of the indoctrination process was the giving of replacement names (7). It is significant how this happens when people seek to destroy an identity and remake it. The name is one of man's most personal and precious possessions. Take it away, and identity suffers a crisis. Give a new name, and a new identity is more easily built. All their Jewish names involved a reference to God. The new names were silent about him and removed him further from their thinking.

Daniel and his friends could, no doubt, have rationalized the situation. They could have got over their disappointments and thrown themselves into their new way of life with zest. Why put up a fight? What use would it be? Who were they against such powerful forces? Best just to go along and comply with everything required of them. Later, once in a position of influence, they could maybe change a few things – that is if they still remembered what they wanted to change. But Daniel and his friends did not play it that way.

They never allowed themselves to forget that the land they now lived in was 'the land of Shinar' – a deliberately old-fashioned name for Babylonia which emphasized that originally it was the place where the Tower of Babel, the symbol of man's opposition to God, was built. They could never allow themselves to be completely at home in such a situation. What, then, were they to do?

One thing they did *not* do was to withdraw completely and refuse to have anything to do with Babylonian culture. There were many good things they could appreciate as there are many good things we can appreciate about our own society, some of which, like freedom, are side effects of secularization. They took their places in Nebuchadnezzar's university and began to study the language and literature of the Babylonians. But that was far from innocent. It necessarily involved the study of magic, sorcery, charms and astrology. Babylonian literature was steeped in it. There they would have learnt anything but a Jewish interpretation of the world and its creation. What a dangerous course of action! Had these things been taught in a religious education class, all their senses would have been primed and they would have been ready for it and ready to reject it. But why should Satan bother with a frontal attack when he can more subtly undermine faith in a literature or history class without anyone realizing it? Daniel and the others took the risk. They were secure enough in their own faith to do so.

Some would have thought that the path of compromise. The practices which the literature spoke of had long been banned in Israel (Deut 18:10–12) and the stricter Jews may have thought them guilty by association. But Daniel and his friends saw no reason to cut themselves off from all mainline culture, providing they could be discriminating about it. To know it and to understand it does not mean to say that you have to believe it.

What was important was that they knew where to draw the line. They chose to draw it when it came to eating food from the king's table (8). Evidently they were prepared to swallow the teaching but not the meals. They asked permission not to eat and proposed an alternative plan. Apparently their winsome behaviour had already softened up the official in charge, and he was obviously prepared to bend over backwards to accommodate them if at all possible. The situation was made easier by the test they proposed. After ten days of their diet they would submit themselves for examination, confident that their God would not let them down.

The reason they drew the line at eating was not just because of Jewish dietary laws. Many of the laws were unenforcible in exile anyway. Rather, it was because joining in a meal said something different than listening to a course of lectures. Meals imply fellowship and agreement – academic training does not. Eating together, even more so then than now, implies a relationship between those who eat. Friendship, family, commitment are involved. To eat would have been to imply that they were agreeing with everything that was being done. If they had compromised on that issue the whole of their distinctiveness as Jews would have crumbled.

They had seen that the meal had symbolic significance. The food may have been unobjectionable in itself, although it probably would have involved them in breaking their laws. What it came to stand for was not unobjectionable. Every generation of Christians living in the exile of a secular environment needs to be alert to the symbols which would involve them in crossing the line. Things which are quite harmless in themselves, such as a salute, a flag, a song, might at certain times take on a new meaning, and that new symbolic importance might mean that Christians have to say 'No' in order to maintain their distance.

Perhaps Sunday trading was such an issue. By refusing to co-operate with a society which is more and more being sold out to mammon, where commercial activity reigns supreme, no matter what spiritual, social and personal costs are involved, Christians who opposed the Sunday Trading Bill may have drawn the line in the right place. They were, in effect, saying to our society that although there is much Christians can appreciate and benefit from, there was a point beyond which they were not prepared to go. Sunday symbolically points men beyond commercialism, greed and materialism. To have given in there would have been to allow secularism to go on its triumphant course unhindered.

Other symbols could be identified, and Christians ought to agree together as to where the line is to be drawn. A whole range of moral and ethical behaviour should mark us out as distinctive. Even things which may be neutral in themselves should be avoided by Christians from time to time, so that the onslaught on secularism can be stopped in its tracks.

We can surely draw that line with the same confidence as Daniel, who knew that he had nothing to lose by standing up for his principles. He was an Old Testament forerunner of Eric Liddell, of *Chariots of Fire* fame. If we believe in the rightness of our Christian position, we should be prepared to put it to a practical test.

Really believing in God (chapter 2)

It was not long before Daniel found himself in another unenviable position. The king had a dream and wanted at least one of his numerous astrologers to interpret it for him. When they could not do so they were condemned to death. The sentence was not just a fit of royal pique. They were condemned because the king feared that they were plotting his overthrow and their silence was all part of the intrigue. Daniel was classed among these so-called wise men.

After consulting with his friends (17) and pleading for God's mercy (18), Daniel decided to put his head on the chopping block. He ventured on to the scaffold only because he really did believe that he had a living God who actively intervened in his world. God was no distant, absentee landlord. Rather, he was the God who changed times and seasons, let kings reign and equally deposed them, gave wisdom to the wise, revealed deep and hidden things and knew the secrets of the dark mysteries which were impenetrable to man (20–23). When Daniel read his newspaper headlines he knew there was more to current affairs than met the eye. Do we?

Then with amazing courage he went off to see Nebuchadnezzar. The dream was about the fall of Nebuchadnezzar's empire and the passing of the three empires which would follow it. No details were given as to how or when the events would take place. The real significance of the dream is not to be found in crystal ball gazing but in three things Daniel had to say.

Firstly he calls Nebuchadnezzar 'the king of kings' (37). And he was not merely being polite to save his skin. He believed it. Nebuchadnezzar had real power in the world, both over mankind and over nature. There was no point in trying to devalue it or deny it. Let us not fool ourselves, such authority does need to be recognized for what it is. The empires which were to follow would equally have real control over the destinies of men and animals.

But secondly, the power was only his because God had given it to him. 'The God of heaven has given you dominion and power and might and glory' (37). It was not his personal possession. He was not a self-made man. Powerful though he might have been from a human viewpoint, he was in a precarious position from a divine standpoint. At any moment God might have chosen to alter the course of events and Nebuchadnezzar would have been powerless to resist. We are too easily fooled into thinking of political power as the ultimate power. Daniel puts it in perspective. Even a pagan king is under the sovereign control of God. Neither Moscow nor Peking, Washington, London or Paris can keep God out, even if they want to.

Thirdly, kingdoms may rise and kingdoms may fall, but there is a kingdom coming 'that will never be destroyed' (44). The kingdom of God is the true reality. This empire will one day strike back, and all the other kingdoms put together will be powerless to defend themselves. All the world's future was to be shaped and moulded according to the purposes of God and the unveiling of his reign. What, then, of all the boasted pomp and circumstance of earthly kingdoms? We think them so secure, so great, so powerful. In reality they fall to a carpenter from Nazareth.

Daniel verbally claimed all life to be under the control of God. God could not be exiled from his world. Nor should our silence let him be. Daniel serves as a pattern for people in the most secular of spheres. We need to stand and claim the ground for God with the same courage and integrity.

Defying the idols (chapter 3)

The lesson Nebuchadnezzar had learnt was soon forgotten. He quickly displaced God and reoccupied the centre of the stage himself. He did so by building a massive statue of himself and demanding that everyone should bow down and worship it. It is amazing how gullible people are, but most seem to have fallen for it, especially the civil servants and military leaders who would have stood to lose more than their jobs if they had defied the king's orders (1–7). Three men, however, had both the courage and the sense to defy the command.

Shadrach, Meshach and Abednego showed a healthy independence of mind. We would have understood if they had given in and bowed in conformity to the social pressure. They could have advanced all sorts of reasons for doing so: their resistance would have been useless; they had responsible positions and couldn't rock the boat; they were prisoners in a foreign land and when in Rome . . . ; politically they were bound to obey; everyone was doing it; they could achieve more by being alive than being dead; they didn't have to believe that the idol was God just because they bowed to it.

The arrogance of their position is fully emphasized in the way the story is told in Daniel. When summoned before the king to explain their behaviour, they say to him, 'O Nebuchadnezzar, we have no need to defend ourselves before you in this matter' (16). Had he ever been spoken to like that before? 'No need'? Did they not realize who he was? Yes, they did. But they believed in a higher authority and greater power. It was the living God of heaven whom they feared, not Nebuchadnezzar.

In interrogating them, Nebuchadnezzar asks a revealing question. 'What god', he queries, 'will be able to rescue you from my hand?' (15). Not only does the question reveal his own naked self-confidence, it also suggests, sadly, that he lived in a world without windows. He could not see God. Never mind, he was about to have the curtains drawn back, the windows cleaned and his vision to the beyond brought into sharper focus than ever before. All because three men were prepared to defy him.

Shadrach, Meshach and Abednego had confidence in God

in two respects. They believed that he had the ability to deliver them from the blazing furnace for which they were bound ('the God we serve is able to save us from it') and that he would intervene on their behalf ('and he will rescue us from your hand'; 17). But what was to come was even more staggering. 'But even if he does not, we want you to know, O king, that we will not serve your gods or worship at the image of gold you have set up' (18). What breathtaking stubbornness! But it takes audacity like that to defy the powerful idols of our man-centred world.

As it was, God's purposes on this occasion were served not by their martyrdom but by their deliverance. So Nebuchadnezzar was made to come to terms with real power. He had humbly to recognize 'the Most High God' (26).

In our secular world it is as difficult for people to see the Most High God as it was for Nebuchadnezzar, because they too are bowing down before the idols. The idols are different and certainly more sophisticated. The mind, technology, money, sex, power, status, success, even health and the family are our contemporary deities. They are idols all the same. Like Shadrach, Meshach and Abednego we need to learn to defy them. We should thumb our noses at them and refuse to let them exercise power over us. We should debunk them and expose their emptiness.

Only as we adopt radically alternative attitudes will we draw back the curtains of secularism and assist people to see the living God beyond. It is time for Christians to revolt, not simply about declining moral standards, but about the tyranny of the rat race, the imperialism of economics and the totalitarianism of secularism. We, too, need to be people of unbending principle, of unwavering confidence and of unswerving loyalty to the living God.

Indicting the world (chapter 4)

Nebuchadnezzar had been dreaming again! Once more it was Daniel to the rescue (8). No one else could interpret the dream for him. The dream consisted of a large tree, reaching to the heavens, in which all kinds of birds and beasts found shelter. But the tree was cut down, its branches were stripped, its fruit scattered and the animals and the birds fled. Only the stump remained, encased in bronze and iron. The dream concluded with mysterious words being spoken by the messenger from heaven which obviously concerned the future of an individual (15, 16).

As soon as Daniel realized what the dream meant he was terrified. How do you tell a king that for seven years he is going to go insane, lose his kingdom and live like an animal? The fact that his kingdom would be restored to him, once his time was up, didn't help very much. Daniel mustered all the tact he could (19) but it was one of those occasions where there really is no way to break the bad news gently. The mental illness which Nebuchadnezzar was to suffer was God's punishment for his wickedness and oppression. Nebuchadnezzar was given the chance to renounce his evil and throw himself on the mercy of God (27), but apparently he did not take it. Twelve months later the illness struck him.

The root cause of Nebuchadnezzar's trouble was pride. 'Is not this the great Babylon I have built as the royal residence, by my mighty power and for the glory of my majesty?' (30). At one level Nebuchadnezzar's claim could not be contradicted. He had been responsible for building an immense and beautiful city. He had built the seven-tiered ziggurat, the wide processional way, the gateway of Ishtar and the double defence walls. Some of his achievements were classed among the seven wonders of the ancient world. He obviously had intended it as a monument to himself. Like Sir Christopher Wren's tomb in St Paul's Cathedral, Nebuchadnezzar was saying, 'If you want to see my monument, look around you.'

At another level, however, it was not true. He had probably never even lifted a trowel or chiselled a stone. Others had done it for him. It had been built by oppressive slave labour. He had used and abused other people for his own ends. His labourers might well have seen his claim in a different light. It was for his oppression of them that Nebuchadnezzar was now being judged.

But at a still deeper level Nebuchadnezzar had got the claim wrong. The whole premiss on which Nebuchadnezzar was building his boast was false. His life was fundamentally adrift. In spite of his previous encounters with the living God he was still living as if God did not exist. God was simply omitted from his picture. He had left God out of his reckoning all along or he would not have been able to oppress people as he did. And once the task was finished he continued to ignore God. There was no humility, no understanding that he was only king as long as God permitted it, and no recognition that God does not share his glory with another.

Daniel had to prick the bubble. He had to cut Nebuchadnezzar down to size. Secularism still exalts man to a supreme position. And the bubble still needs pricking. On every hand we see men making the same foolish boasts as Nebuchadnezzar did. Sadly, too, we see the same consequences of such a false premiss wherever we look. Men are still oppressed by others in the cause of economic progress, political power or social prestige. When you leave God out, that's what happens. Like Daniel, we still need to put the world in the dock and accuse it of the crime of which it is guilty.

Writing on the wall (chapter 5)

The events of Daniel 5 have often been used as the basis of evangelistic preaching. In reality, however, it deals not with individual conversion but the downfall of an empire. One of Nebuchadnezzar's successors, King Belshazzar, was presiding over the decline of the Babylonian empire without even realizing it.

The whole society had gone to seed. Pleasure-seeking drunken orgies were the order of the day. And during these decadent displays the sacred objects of Israel's religion were obscenely devalued and used by the pagans as mere drinking tankards (3).

There was no respect for the living God. They could rise no higher than to worship gold and silver, bronze, iron, wood and stone (4).

It's hard to communicate with men who are engulfed by self-indulgent luxury. God therefore chose a dramatic way of doing so. Writing on the wall with the fingers of a human hand which appear out of nowhere is not God's normal method of communication! But sometimes God has to resort to out-of-the-ordinary methods to penetrate our thick secular skins, such as when a tragedy strikes, when the bottom drops out of a person's world or when people encounter the puzzling interruption of the supernatural in their mundane lives.

Belshazzar was eager to have this unusual phenomenon explained. And Daniel found himself again the bearer of an unwelcome message. It is interesting to see what is said of Daniel: 'There is a man in your kingdom who has the spirit of the holy gods in him' (11). Now there is poor theology if you like! Didn't they know there was only one God? In such circumstances the niceties of theology do not matter. The point is that when there is a real need people know where to turn. Daniel, from their viewpoint, had that indefinable something which marked him out as different, and when they had come to an end of themselves and had discovered how bankrupt their own resources were, when they wanted a word of wisdom, then they knew where to go. We often find ourselves in situations when the last thing we should do is to argue theology, for the simple reason that we are being presented with an open door to talk for God rather than about him.

Daniel did just that. The empire was about to come to a sudden end and its downfall was an act of God's judgment.

God moved against it for three reasons. Belshazzar had reigned in pride and had shown no humility. He had failed to learn from his father's experience. Secondly, he had used religious objects, and so the God of whom they spoke, to his own ends (23). Thirdly, he had worshipped idols and did not acknowledge that there was a living God who held all his life and his ways in his hand (23). Consequently his days were numbered; he had been tried and found wanting and his kingdom was about to be lost and divided (26–28). Almost before the king could say Nebuchadnezzar, Daniel's words came true. The very night of the show-down was the last night of Belshazzar's life – and of the Babylonian empire.

It is both as individuals and as societies that we are in danger if we live secular lives. Leave God out and there comes a time when he pronounces his verdict and executes his sentence. The tragedies come, the unexplained happens, the world falls apart. It is always happening. It is a recurring process within history and within families. And when it happens God needs his spokesmen in the right place, ready to explain; men of wisdom who are recognized as having 'the spirit of the holy gods' within them.

Continuing the battle (chapter 6)

The government changed and Daniel might have wished for an honourable retirement from the spiritual battle. But it was not to be. There are no Old Age Pensioners in God's work. Truth to tell, his worst ordeal was yet to come. Daniel was known as a man of such integrity that his colleagues could find no fault in him (4). Darius, the new ruler, would have been wise to use Daniel as a respected elder statesman. It would have done much for race relations and for the harmony of his newly acquired territories. But good men are not always appreciated, especially by bad men. True to life, Daniel, as a good man, provoked an ambiguous response. Some respected him and others hated him, while some men did both at the same time. Though Darius himself had personal regard for Daniel, many of his advisers were looking for a chance to stick a knife in his back. So, unwittingly, Darius allowed himself to be manipulated to the extent that Daniel could fall foul to one of his own laws and be sentenced to death by being thrown into a den of lions.

Once more, the root of the problem lay in the king usurping the place of God. Darius was persuaded to enact a law that for thirty days no one should pray to any God or man except him. Darius apparently felt himself worthy of men's worship and capable of answering all their petitions. He was claiming to be all-powerful. True believers, like Daniel, simply could not obey. The issue was black and white. There were no shades of grey when it came to such blasphemy.

Daniel's defiance was deliberate and calculated. He knew well the cost which would be involved, but he was prepared for that. His defiance was open but not ostentatious. In his own home he went upstairs to a window which looked towards Jerusalem and there knelt to pray (10). He did not invite the local press corps around for a posed photo session. But neither did he hide his light under a bucket.

His defiance was persistent. He prayed three times a day. Here was no politician engaged in token action, ready to retreat to safety once he had made his half-hearted stand. Daniel's prayer was not a political gesture, but an expression of his lifelong spiritual practice. He could only have kept going in such circumstances because he had years of walking with God, none of which he regretted, to sustain him.

The intelligence network got to work and Daniel was soon ensnared. Darius found himself in a catch-22 situation. Heads, and Daniel, whom he loved, lost his head in a den of lions. Tails, and there would be a tale to be told about a king who did not have the stamina to carry through his own laws. He may not have wanted to throw Daniel to the lions, but he had no choice in the matter. His own stupid law condemned him to action that he could see was patently unjust.

Once in the den, however, the living God intervened.

Significantly, the living God was able to do what Darius, the pretender to deity could not do. Darius could not deliver Daniel from the lion's den, but God could. That soon showed who was in charge and worthy of worship.

Darius had the honesty to express his joy when Daniel was delivered. People usually are delighted when truth wins and right is done. They gain a new respect for God when prayer is answered.

It is not clear how far Darius was 'converted' through the incident. Certainly he urged toleration and insisted that the religion of the Jews should not be harassed (26). From his subsequent remarks he may have gone further. He claimed the God of Daniel to be the living God who endures for ever, whose kingdom would never be destroyed and who rescues and saves, doing signs and wonders both in heaven and on earth (26, 27).

But the uncertainty of his response is true to life as well. God sometimes remarkably intervenes in our world and people see it and are astonished. They gain a new respect for the Christian faith and may even make bold claims or promises. But in spite of that, they are not always genuinely converted and their commitment to God may not be sustained. That is just the way it is. But the important thing is that God has erected another question mark in our secular world. He has placed another comma, which slows the world down in its headlong rush into unbelief.

Conclusion

God needs people in high places. How thankful the Jews must have been that Daniel, Shadrach, Meshach and Abednego did not withdraw from society. They were not interested in stainless-steel holiness, that is, holiness which keeps itself clean at all costs but which is cold and indifferent to real needs. They were prepared to get stuck in to the difficult and mucky situations of their world and to work out their holiness at the sharp end of things.

In our secular world, we dare not withdraw in a futile attempt to preserve our own purity. Christians need to be involved in all sections of society. God needs people at the top, influencing government, industry, education and entertainment. But he needs them in the gutters, picking up the broken and bruised of our society as well. The social setting in which the call of God is worked out will be different for each one of us. But what matters is whether we are prepared to live like Daniel wherever God puts us.

We can only do so if we believe as he did. He really did believe that God was in control; that he was sovereign over all life and could be excluded from none of it; that he was capable of intervening in a world which was not a closed system; that he was more powerful than idols and that he was more important than anything, even life itself.

That belief led him to action. He accepted what he could, but he knew where to draw the line. He was always courteous, and yet never minced his words. He did not hold back, but courageously spoke of God in a world which had different ideas from those funny Jews about divinity. He and his friends stood firm, regardless of the consequences. Although they had some close shaves, God chose to deliver them. It will not always be the case that God does so. But Christians must stand firm as a matter of principle, not because they can be sure of the consequences. They were prepared openly to defy the gods and the decrees of their world, showing them the disrespect they deserved.

It is easy enough to relate all this to totalitarian regimes where Christians are persecuted and state law is blatantly anti-God. But we need to be as perceptive about the so-called Christian West where the totalitarian noose of secularism is tightening all the time. We are not called to any different sort of discipleship from our brethren in the days of Daniel, or in the atheist nations of our time.

9
Living as pilgrims: Hebrews 11

Christians are for ever condemned to live as pilgrims. That is, they never quite belong to the world in which they live – they never quite fit. They are not holiday-makers. They have a sense of purpose and a direction which the holiday-maker lacks. They are intent on getting to know God. But precisely because that is their aim they must sit loose to the world in which they live and will often question its dominant values. There is much about the world they can enjoy and much in which they can be involved. But they are never more than pilgrims.

No part of the New Testament illustrates this teaching more than the letter to the Hebrews and particularly Hebrews 11. There the writer draws lessons from a number of Old Testament characters who stood against the prevailing secularism of their own day. In their primitive way they have much to teach us about coping with a world which is alien in its world-view. They put down markers and give us directions. They show how they tackled the issues raised in chapter seven of this book. Before looking at the specific individuals it may be helpful to set them in the wider context of the letter.

Hebrews was probably written to a group of Jewish converts who were beginning to feel that their conversion had been a mistake. Becoming a Christian would have cut them loose from their social moorings and caused them quite a bit of insecurity. Many of their family and a lot of their friends would have found it difficult to appreciate their decision. What was wrong with the old religion? In rejecting Judaism, to some extent they were inevitably rejecting its followers at the same time. Perhaps some were beginning to suspect that a return to the religion of their fathers would be good – it would overcome the hassles they had experienced. So the author spends a good deal of time comparing the Jewish and Christian faiths, point by point, and proving the superiority of Jesus to anything Judaism had to offer.

But the unsettlement had a deeper dimension as well. Having cut loose from their inherited religion, some were wondering whether they should cut loose from religion altogether. Was it really worth it? Could it really be proved? Why bother? To answer these questions the writer engages in a brilliant analysis of faith. Its teaching has never been more relevant than today, when the tide of belief has gone out and many Christians feel that they have been washed up on the shore of secularism.

Back to basics: what faith is

In talking of faith, Hebrews takes nothing for granted. It begins at the beginning so that the Christians can be sure that their foundations are good.

What is faith? It is not a half-hearted 'think so' approach to religion or the 'I hope so' sentiment which we adopt when longing for the weather to be fine for the Sunday school picnic. Nor is it wishful thinking or false consciousness. Still less is it the pathetic defence mechanism we sometimes use when we refuse to believe the truth about an illness or a broken marriage and say we have hope when we know we have none. Faith is a conviction, a settled determination to go on obeying God, no matter what. That's why the writer says, 'Now faith is being sure of what we hope for . . .' (11:1).

And yet faith deals in a different tense and a different dimension to that in which people normally operate. It pits the future against the present. It banks on there being something beyond this life. If we were only ever to live within the limits of what we could experience today life would be a very poor thing. We would never save to get married, never work to pass exams, never plant a garden for the future, never spend time researching to solve a problem. Much of the best activity in life is enriching simply because it allows some future hope to dictate the way we behave in the present.

The Christian differs from the secularist in that he is more far-sighted. He not only allows his own uncertain future on this earth to determine how he behaves but he allows his much more certain future after this life to dictate his pattern in life. Life here is uncertain. None of us knows whether we shall survive tomorrow or not. What is not uncertain is that we shall all die and that after death there will be a resurrection in which we shall all participate. The resurrection of Jesus guarantees that. Christians therefore allow the thought of meeting their maker to govern the way they live now.

The different dimension means that the Christian allows the unseen to rule the seen. To put that another way, faith means that we interpret life spiritually and not simply according to the senses.

The things that are seen consist of balance sheets, economic realities, political power, social prestige, military might, technological achievements and so on. But what is unseen, in a word, is God. It is characteristic of him to work in the dimension of the unseen. Indeed, the very real seen world of which we are all so conscious was formed from the invisible in the first place (11:3). So there are values, goals, powers, authorities, causes and effects which are not open to scientific investigation. But they are no less real. The man of faith takes these into account in the way in which he lives.

Since everything about our world says that it is only the seen which is real, it is a battle to live the life of faith. As the German pastor and theologian Helmut Thielicke has put it, 'Believing is by no means a question of what I believe in, but always a question of against what I believe. For faith must always struggle against appearances.'

What does the life of faith achieve? Commendation by God (see, for example, 11: 2, 4, 5.). Deep down, each one of us wants to be accepted and to belong. Think of all the things we do in order to be accepted by our peers. We wear the latest fashions, we buy the latest gadgets, we speak the latest language. We would do almost anything to avoid their disapproval and find ourselves on the outside. If only we were as serious about being approved by God as we are about earning the commendation of our peers! The life of faith means we have a clear goal – to be commended by God – and that we bend every effort to achieve it. Doing so may well cost us the approval of our fellow men, but although that hurts and matters to us, such rejection is trivial in comparison with gaining God's disapproval. He matters more than them.

Just in case his readers have failed to grasp the point, the author includes a single verse about Abel and Cain (11:4). Abel went all out for God's approval. It earned him Cain's disapproval and lost him his life. But no matter. What God thought was more important than what Cain thought, and even more important than life itself.

In his description of faith the writer is careful to use another significant word. He says that 'By faith we *understand* that the universe was formed at God's command . . .' (11:3). Once more the Bible is at pains to stress that faith is not a matter of being gullible or credulous but involves the mind. Faith has to do with evidence just as much as secularism does. But it has to do with evidence which takes

God into account rather than shutting and bolting the door against him. The Christian interprets the same evidence as the secularist does, but is more open than the secularist will ever be. It is the secularist who is narrow-minded, not the Christian. But the Christian must use his mind, which, sadly, he has not always done. He must not believe because 'it feels right' or because some persuasive preacher, who doesn't know what he is talking about, has said it, or simply because it seems more sensational than anything else and so must come from God. Discernment is necessary and everything is to be tested.

Like many other writers in scripture, the author to the Hebrews believes that the best way to teach his lesson is to teach it by example. So let's now look at the gang of four, the big characters he deals with in Hebrews 11 to illustrate the meaning of faith.

Enoch: walking with God

Enoch lived just seven generations after Adam, yet his world was one already dominated by unbelief. Jude 16 reports him as saying of his contemporaries, 'These men are grumblers and fault-finders; they follow their own evil desires; they boast about themselves and flatter others for their own advantage.' They would never have lived such self-centred and sensual lives if they had believed in God.

Enoch stood out as different because he did believe that God existed (11:6). You can just imagine the ridicule he must have attracted. But it didn't deter him. With simple logic, Enoch reckoned that if God existed then it was more important than anything to earn God's approval. So he set out to cultivate God's companionship.

There is no short cut to cultivating the friendship of God. You can only do it as you spend much time in his company. You cannot do it by inviting God in for an occasional cup of coffee out of some sense of obligation to be hospitable. You must invite him in frequently and spend hours with him because you want to learn to enjoy his company.

The delightful way in which the Old Testament puts it is that 'Enoch walked with God 300 years' (Gen 5:22). It's a simple way of talking about companionship. But 300 years is a long time. It must have involved discipline to keep going that long when everyone else thought you were mad to believe that there even was a God, and it certainly gave you some exercise!

But time is of the essence in cultivating any friendship. As Dean Inge once perceptively quizzed, 'If we spend sixteen hours a day dealing with tangible things and only a few minutes with God, is it any wonder that the tangible things are 200 times more real than God?' A W Tozer put it, bluntly, 'The man who would know God must give him time.'

If we are to maintain our belief in spite of our unbelieving environment we must be prepared to give God time. The spiritual dimension will only become real when we give it the same careful attention as the material dimension. We will be riddled with doubt and uncertainty, and swayed by the present and the seen, if we do not.

One day Enoch went out for his walk and never came back. (A Sunday school girl explained it like this: 'One day Enoch and God went out for a walk together and they got so far away from Enoch's home that God said to him, "We're nearer my home than yours, why don't you come home to tea?" And he did.') What a puzzle that must have caused. They probably sent out their search parties. They may have pitied him or even been angry with him for not returning. But they must have wondered, too, what his disappearance meant.

'I see nobody on the road,' said Alice.

'I only wish I had such eyes,' the King remarked in a fretful tone. 'To be able to see Nobody! And at such a distance too! Why, it is as much as I can do to see real people by this light.'

The unbeliever may well deride the Christian in a different tone from that of the King to Alice. His misunder-

standing may not have been genuine, but we need to see
'Nobody' on the road and then walk with him, into eternity.

Noah: witnessing for God

Noah was a risk-taker. He risked everything because of his
belief in God. Had he not done so he would have lost
everything, as many do. Many in his day, as in ours, tried
to conserve what they had. Preserving present and seen
possessions seems more sensible than allowing your life to
be shaped by an unseen future. But those who take that
course of action usually find their faith oozes out of them
like toothpaste out of a tube. Noah was alone in his generation in being in step with God (Gen 6:9). Being in step
with God meant that his ear was tuned into God when
others simply could not hear his voice.

Charles Swindoll, the American pastor and author,
mentions in his book on Ecclesiastes, *Living on the Ragged
Edge*, an Indian walking in New York City who stopped
his friend and said that he could hear a cricket. His friend
thought him mad. How could he hear a cricket with all the
noise of city life around him? But sure enough, a block
away, the Indian found the cricket he had heard. Asked
how he could possibly have heard it, the Indian said, 'Well,
my ears are different from yours. It simply depends on what
you are listening to.' Then he proceeded to demonstrate. He
took some coins from his pocket and dropped them on the
pavement. Every head nearby turned around and looked in
the direction of the Indian! It all depends what you are
listening for.

Noah was listening for God and he refused to allow the
evil environment in which he lived to jam the radio waves
from eternity. All that others could hear was the noise of
the world around them, a din they were making themselves.
What Noah heard was that his present world order was
under God's condemnation. As the Bible says, he was
'warned about things not yet seen' (11:7).

But there is no point in listening unless you act on what you hear. Noah acted even though it meant building an ark in the middle of a desert. What a crazy thing to do! We know his action caused derisive laughter among his friends. Well, how would you have reacted? They had never seen a boat, still less a flood. They had no marine architects or surveyors or boat-builders around to give advice. Even if there was a flood, how would this amateur floating structure survive when it had not had the benefit of man's technological know-how while it was being built? And they simply could not understand Noah's reason for building this structure.

Noah spoke to them about God, about the future and about judgment, but they did not find him intelligible. He might as well have been speaking a different language. What is more, there was no way in which he could prove anything to them. By its very nature the only convincing proof was the flood itself. And by the time the proof came and the downpour started, it was too late for them to do anything about it.

So Noah did not fit easily into his society. Life was uncomfortable for him. But he had true reality on his side, for while other people were motivated by the attractive things of this world he was motivated by 'holy fear' (7). The opinions of others would soon be forgotten, but in the end God was the great reality whose opinion was the only one that really counted for anything.

His faith had a twofold result. On the one hand it led to the salvation of his family. The risk had paid off. On the other hand his very action was a further condemnation of the world (7). The water which supported Noah and his family, drowned others.

Salvation and judgment are two sides of the same coin. For some to be saved, others must be lost. For the oppressed to be set free, the oppressors must be overthrown. For the good to be rewarded, evil ones must be punished. They cannot coexist.

Here is the truth about witnessing for God. It not only

involves the lonely task of speaking for God but also requires that we speak against the world. It means we speak both good news and bad news. By their faith, the people of God serve as a witness for the prosecution of the world, just as Jesus came into the world and the world added to its own condemnation because it rejected him. So it is to be with all pilgrims. Our role is to speak eternal truth and invite men to join us in believing it. When they don't, the judgment is on their own heads. So let's not bend over backwards to be polite to secularism and try to do all we can to accommodate it. It is in the process of inviting God's judgment.

Abraham: waiting on God

No one in the Bible illustrates the pilgrimage of faith more clearly than Abraham. For him it meant leaving the security of everything with which he was familiar and being cast adrift in an unknown sea with only God to pilot him. Frankly, 'he did not know where he was going' (8) and when he got there he never really settled. The nearest he ever got to belonging anywhere was to live 'like a stranger in a foreign country', erecting and dismantling his tents (9). He never put his roots down, never dug any foundations and never even mortgaged a semi next to some nice, friendly Canaanite. The largest thing he ever owned was a parcel of land big enough to take his wife's coffin when she died (Gen 23: 6–9, 17–20).

One of the surest marks that God is at work in us is when we begin to cut loose from the things which the world counts as so important. That does not mean to say that we should all be world-rejecters. It does mean that we must find our security in God alone.

What motivated Abraham was not the present but the future: 'He was looking forward to the city with foundations, whose architect and builder is God' (11:10). That was the greater reality which moulded his thinking. Better to invest in such a good builder and wise architect than to throw your money away down here. Earthly foundations crumble and buildings decay. Cities die or are destroyed. Fashions change and planning decisions can blight an area. But faith gives you the eyes to see into the future and to see that there is a building society in which it is far more worthwhile to invest. For God is building a city that will last. True, you have to wait a little while for a return on your capital. But when it comes, it is at a higher interest rate than anything you can receive down here.

Faith not only led him to be patient in terms of waiting for the heavenly city but also led him to be patient about a matter much closer to home as well. God had not only promised a city but a family. Now Abraham was no chicken when he left Ur, he was seventy-five years old. It was then God promised him a son! Eleven years later a child was born, but it was not the child of promise. Abraham had found it hard to wait so he had tried to force God's hand. He bore a son by a slave woman called Hagar rather than by Sarah, his wife. But God was teaching him that faith was all about patience.

God kept Abraham waiting another fourteen years before Isaac, the child of promise was born. What agony that wait must have been as month in and month out for all those years their hopes of a child were dashed again. Not only was he 100 years old when it eventually happened, but Sarah was long-since past child-bearing age, even if she had not been infertile all her life. It was impossible. Just imagine what the neighbours would have said when Sarah began to look pregnant. How they must have gossiped and talked of fantasy pregnancies! But the art of the possible is politics. Faith is the art of the impossible.

Faith meant that Abraham had to keep believing when everything around him cried that it was futile. J O Sanders has pointed out that, 'Faith is frequently called upon to run in double harness with patience.' Faith is faithfulness. Faith comes into play when the evidence is weak; when the miracles don't happen; when the signs and wonders are absent. As Bishop Mervyn Stockwood said to David Watson during his prolonged illness, 'The greatest test of the Christian life is to live with the silences of God.' So it is. But that's faith.

At last the child of promise was born and God proved true to his word. But it wasn't just that one child was born. From this one old man, and him as good as dead, a great nation was born (11:12).

Then the craziest thing happened. Abraham was told by God to take this child, for whom he had been waiting all these years, and murder him. Dressing it up as a religious sacrifice didn't really help to soften the blow. Murder is murder, whatever the setting. What absurdity! What self-contradiction! What a torrent of bewildered emotion must have cascaded through Abraham's elderly mind. What a waste of God's gift. Had God made a mistake? Was God punishing him for something he had done? Did God really want to make them go through the baby-bearing episode all over again? Worst of all, had God changed his mind? Was he not going to be true to his promise after all?

Abraham could have argued it all out and rationalized God's command somehow. But the point is that if God has said it, faith accepts even what it cannot understand.

From the way the story is told in Genesis 22 it appears that Abraham made his way ungrudgingly to Mount Moriah and was ready to sacrifice his son there. Hebrews sheds light on why Abraham took it all so calmly. It says, 'Abraham reasoned that God could raise the dead . . .' (11:19). At long last Abraham had passed his examination in faith. All his life he had failed because he thought he was more capable of working things out than God was. At last he had learnt that God's methods were so much better than his own. So why not just do as he was told? His own experience told him that God was capable of doing the impossible. The child had once been born from a lifeless womb, so why, if God so wished, could he not be received back to life from a lifeless corpse?

A secular environment may be a very barren environment

for the Christian. There may be times when we think that God could give us more help than he does, when we wish he would intervene more frequently, speak more clearly or act more quickly. But faith means waiting for God in spite of the perplexities of our own experience. And in a world given to instant answers that is not easy.

Moses: warfare for God

Bill Grant's hobby is trying to track down the yeti. Before he went on a recent expedition to Tibet, he responded to a BBC interviewer in these memorable words, 'Only those who can see the invisible can do the impossible.' Liberating the children of Israel from their slavery in Egypt was impossible. But Moses did it because he had seen the invisible.

Emerson defined faith like this: 'Faith is the rejection of a lesser fact and the acceptance of a greater fact. God is the greater fact. Whatever else impinges on my consciousness, I know he is. I know he cares.' Moses's life was dominated by some pretty impressive facts – like the attraction of the Egyptian court, the scheming of his family, the muscle of the Egyptian army, the cunning of the secret service, the price tag on his own head as a fugitive from justice and the dispirited argumentativeness of his own people. But there was a greater fact than all that, namely God. An encounter with God while Moses was an obscure shepherd without any hopes of going anywhere changed everything.

Faith turned his world upside down. It caused him to reject the status symbols of the world. He refused to be known as the son of Pharoah's daughter (11:24). The things which his world defined as worthwhile, no longer exercised any influence over him. Hand in hand with that rejection went an acceptance of suffering. 'He chose to be ill-treated along with the people of God . . .' (11:25). He chose to identify with the oppressed of the world and not simply to express his sympathy for them. In doing so he was engaging in behaviour which had a deeper meaning than he could have imagined, for by identifying with them he was identifying with Christ: 'He considered the stigma that rests on God's Anointed [ie Christ] greater wealth than the treasures of Egypt' (26, NEB).

So faith caused him to unmask sin and reveal it for the empty short-changing master that it is. Of course it brings some pleasure. If there were no pleasure in sin it would not be a problem. But its pleasures are so short-term. Sin is like a drug. The more you do the more you get hooked. The more you do the more you need to do because its pleasures work according to a law of diminishing returns. One fix needs to be followed at ever-shorter intervals by another. What a sham its pleasures are! Moses turned his back on all that.

What led him to this radical life-style was the greater reality of God (11:26,27). Concern for the future displaced preoccupation with the present. He looked ahead for his reward. Concern with the long-term displaced fear in the short-term. He persevered and did not fear the king's anger. Concern with the unseen displaced the stranglehold of the seen. He persevered because he saw him who was invisible. In Calvin's words, 'The true nature of faith is always to have God before our eyes.'

The perspective of faith led him to obey God in initiating the Passover meal. Analysed from the viewpoint of scientific cause and effect, it makes no sense. How could the killing of an animal and the smearing of its blood on the doorposts possibly help an oppressed people to escape? But it did. God said it, so Moses did it. That's faith.

Faith, for us as well as Moses, must dictate the choices we make in life.

It will cause us, if we approach it with integrity, to come to some radical alternatives which will not be understood in mainline society. We will reject idolatry, accept a sacrificial life-style and turn our back on the sin which the world mistakenly thinks is the only way to find pleasure.

It will cause us to have a totally different perspective on

things. We will not live for the now but in the light of the hereafter. We will not live for the short-term but the long-term. We will not live in the dimension of the seen but of the unseen. It may lead us to some odd action, but in obeying God we will allow him to use us to achieve his ends.

As Hebrews 11:13 points out, none of these men saw the fulfilment of the things they believed in. They could only be sure of them from a distance. While the ultimate fulfilment of our salvation still awaits us, in Christ we have already received so much more than they did. Being surrounded by them, and being able to fix our eyes on Jesus (12:1–3), how much greater should our faith be, in spite of the desert in which we are called to live!

10
Are Christians an endangered species?

Many will conclude that this is a pessimistic book. Secularization is a real threat: Christians are not only embattled but endangered; the chances of their survival are minimal.

Is that true? The answer, bluntly, is that it is no truer now than it has ever been. Christians have often been in just that situation, perhaps more often than not. The form which the attack of secularization now takes may seem as different from previous forms as nuclear weapons seem different from bows and arrows. But we must remember that in their day even bows and arrows were a deadly threat to whole societies.

So what strategy are we going to adopt to deal with the threat? Sociologists have two stark ways of expressing our options. We can either accommodate to secularization or resist it. In reality our response must be a good deal more complicated, but the starkness of the contrast serves to clarify our thinking.

To accommodate or not to accommodate

The secular world-view is not going to go away overnight. It is a major force within our world which cannot be ignored and therefore, many would argue, rather than ignoring it or fighting it, we ought to see where we can form an alliance between our Christian faith and secularism.

Furthermore, there are many good things which have resulted from secularization. We must be grateful for the advances of science and technology which can be seen as an outworking of God's commission to man to 'fill the earth and subdue it' (Gen 1:28).

We must be thankful that research has been freed from the ignorant tyranny of ecclesiastics so that we do not find ourselves any longer in the ludicrous position of Galileo, having to renounce what we know to be patently true because the church says so, inhibited from further investigation.

We should be glad that ministers of religion are now free to concentrate on their spiritual duties and no longer have to serve their communities as doctors, lawyers, teachers and medical officers of health as once they did.

We should be glad that anarchic and superstitious spiritism has been controlled and that there is a greater sense of rationality about our world, reflecting God as an orderly creator who is supreme in his authority over all other spiritual powers.

So why not accept the nature of our world and accommodate to it?

The answer is, 'It all depends what you mean by "accommodate".' By accommodation, many mean assimilation. That is, they start with the secular world and seek to take elements of it into their Christianity. They take the secular world as the starting-point and let it become the judge as to what can be believed and what must be rejected.

So, since modern man finds it difficult to believe in miracles, the Bible has to be demythologized and a faith is created which is denuded of the supernatural. Or, since tolerance is seen as a virtue, it is difficult to believe in a God who will not ultimately tolerate everyone. So belief in judgment and hell are rejected. Or, since the contemporary world sees homosexuality as a legitimate expression of sexuality, the Bible's teaching, which clearly labels it as a sin, is dismissed as a cultural anachronism. A new theology of sexuality is needed which can justify it. Or, the image of the Christian minister must be radically altered to meet the needs of the people in the real world rather than to serve the introverted concerns of his own flock and his narrow piety. So we turn the minister into a welfare officer or disco organizer or a political activist because that is what the secular world demands.

The fatal flaw in this approach is that in the end you have nothing distinctively Christian left. If all you are going to do is to put the secular values of the world into religious language, why bother? People will not turn to the church for what they can get – often in a more professional way – elsewhere unless it has something distinctive to offer. This approach, which starts with the laudable aim of christianizing the world ends with the tragic result of secularizing the church.

Having said that, there is a right sense in which the church must accommodate the secular world. This is not by assimilating it but by adapting to it. The Bible gives us ample encouragement to do so. We have seen the example of the exiled Daniel who did not withdraw but adapted to his new circumstances, accepting much from the hands of the alien government of Babylon. We have seen how the New Testament apostles adapted the language of the gospel to new cultural surroundings. They did not stubbornly persist in calling Jesus the Messiah when communicating the gospel to Gentile audiences. It would have meant nothing to them if they had. Similarly, the forms of their church government and fellowship life adapted to the surroundings in which the church lived.

There is a right sense in which we must learn to adapt.

So much of our language, customs, concerns and organizational life is simply irrelevant to the world in which we live. It is a hindrance to the spreading of the gospel. People will inevitably stumble over the offence of the gospel itself, but these things provide an offence of our own making. In this sense we must adapt and take the good news of Jesus outside of the walls of our churches.

To resist or not to resist

The option of resistance certainly seems to have more to commend it. It does not suffer the fatal flaw of so compromising our faith that we end up with nothing left.

Resistance means that much of the contemporary world's values and interpretations will be rejected. Rather than letting the secular world determine what to believe or how to behave, those who resist judge the world by their Christian faith. The starting-point and the criterion for accepting something as true is not the world but the Faith. So, although modern man may find it hard to believe in the miraculous, or hell, or a strict sexual ethic, or whatever, the Christian will continue to take his stand on these issues. While modern man believes that there are no windows to look out of, the Christian will constantly point to them and be seen to be looking out of them.

There is much support for this position, as this book has argued, within the Bible. True believers have always been in a minority and have had to take their stand against the prevailing views of their day. We stand in that tradition.

Furthermore, recent research lends support to the wisdom of this position. Steve Bruce, in his studies of evangelicalism, has demonstrated how this resistance has helped evangelicalism to survive the unfavourable secular climate while more liberal approaches to faith have not coped so well. Clear ideas about belief, concern to maintain the purity of belief, clear objectives and goals, and strong networks and support structures such as para-church organizations, books, cassettes and conferences, all help.

Even so, the road must not be followed carelessly. Christians have a track record of resisting over the wrong issues, only later to have to admit the folly of their resistance and give in. If we are to resist we must pick the sites of our resistance with care, just as Daniel did. Issues should be major, symbolic and of enduring value. They dare not be cultural issues that are really trivial – there we can adapt. They must be fundamental spiritual matters.

A second danger in resistance is that if we spend all our time resisting we end up as a narrow, negative, declining, inbred group, increasingly out of touch with the world and increasingly only able to talk with each other. There is a danger in not being distinctive enough but there is also a danger in being too distinctive in the wrong way. We need Christian scientists and economists and others who will be fully, but not uncritically, involved in the 'real' world. To cut ourselves off from that will only lead, in the long run, to a great gulf being fixed between the Christian and the non-Christian across which we cannot communicate the love of Christ.

We dare not resist simply to preserve ourselves. We exist for the sake of mission and that demands that we take risks and become vulnerable as we engage with the world. In so doing we are simply being obedient to the pattern of our Lord who became vulnerable in the incarnation.

Adapting and resisting: the twofold calling

We must give due weight to the apparently competing claims of scripture. The Lord's message through Jeremiah is a message to us too: 'Seek the peace and prosperity of the city to which I have carried you into exile. Pray to the Lord for it, because if it prospers, you too will prosper (Jer 29:7). Yet we must equally remember John's message: 'Do not love the world or anything in the world. If anyone loves the world, the love of the Father is not in him . . . The world and its desires pass away, but the man who does the will of God lives for ever' (1 John 2:15,17).

Jesus neatly summed up the tension with which we have to live. We are to be in the world but not of it (John 17:15,16). We are to live with that tension knowing when it is right to adapt and when it is right to resist.

Far from being pessimistic about the survival chances of the Christian species, there are grounds for optimism. There are signs that:

● Secularism is digging its own grave. The world it creates is barren, deficient and discontented. When people have had their fill they will be open in a new way to the good news of Jesus.

● Secularism gives us new opportunities. Having been freed by it from much of the imposed baggage of the civilization of yesteryear we are free in a new way to concentrate on the real missionary calling which is ours.

● Some Christians are working to overcome the divorce between the private world of faith and the public 'real' world. Thank God for the philosophers, politicians, teachers, journalists, artists and entertainers who are putting the God-perspective back into their sphere of work. Thank God too for a growing number of ordinary Christians who witness for Christ and, through the quality of their lives, point beyond themselves to God.

● Christians are increasingly vocal about questions of morality and are prepared to exercise their full democratic rights and claim back some of the ground for God.

● Some Christian groups are growing in strength and vitality because they have not compromised during less promising days but kept clear boundaries and goals. They are now coming into their own.

● Even if the church might be greatly weakened by secularization, it is not a terminal illness from which God can suffer. His life is breaking out in new ways and being expressed through new channels which constantly surprise us.

There is hope that we might transform our nation once more for God. Impossible? Maybe, but the signs read otherwise. There are too few of us? Perhaps. But let me paraphrase the words of one astute observer of our present scene: There are signs of new life in those Christian groups which strongly resist the dominant secular culture. But if they are to succeed in reconverting post-Christian Britain they will have to reverse powerful movements such as secularization and modernization. It would be a transformation of modern industrial society itself. Not a very likely prospect. But neither was it likely, 2,000 years ago, that an insignificant Jewish cult would succeed in turning the great classical world upside down. But it did! What God has done before, he can do again.

For further reading

The Homeless Mind Peter L Berger, Brigitte Berger and Hansfried Kellner (Penguin 1974)

The Christian Mind Harry Blamires (SPCK 1963)

Blind Alley Beliefs David Cook (Pickering and Inglis 1979)

The Making of Post-Christian Britain Alan D Gilbert (Longman 1980)

The Gravedigger File Os Guinness (Hodder and Stoughton 1983)

The Steeple's Shadow David Lyon (SPCK 1985)

Religion in Sociological Perspective Bryan R Wilson (OUP 1982)